Bill Douglas

DATE

Bill Douglas A Lanternist's Account

Edited by Eddie Dick,

Andrew Noble

and Duncan Petrie

BFI Publishing

in association with the

Scottish Film Council

Photograph of Bill Douglas
on title page
by David Appleby

First published in 1993 by the
British Film Institute
21 Stephen Street
London W1P 1PL

British Library Cataloguing-in-Publication Data.
A catalogue record for this book is available
from the British Library.

ISBN 0–85170–347–X
      0–85170–348–8 pbk

Designed by
Andrew Barron & Collis Clements Associates

Typeset in Sabon by
Fakenham Photosetting Limited,
Fakenham, Norfolk

Printed in Great Britain by
BAS Printers Ltd, Over Wallop, Hampshire

The British Film Institute acknowledges subsidy
from the Scottish Arts Council
towards the publication of this volume.

Contents

Acknowledgments   7

Notes on Contributors   9

Foreword Lindsay Anderson   11

Bill Douglas, 1934–1991: A Memoir Andrew Noble   13

The Bill Douglas Trilogy Bill Douglas   29

My Childhood   31

My Ain Folk   55

My Way Home   83

The Making of the Trilogy Andrew Noble   117

The Lanternist Revisited: The Making of 'Comrades'   173
Duncan Petrie

Don't Mourn – Analyse: Reviewing the Trilogy John Caughie   197

Homing Andrew O'Hagan   205

Women in the Bill Douglas Trilogy Joyce McMillan   219

Working with Bill Mamoun Hassan   227

Filmography   233

Acknowledgments

The editors would like to acknowledge the invaluable assistance and support of Peter Jewell without whom this project would have been impossible.

Thanks also to Roma Gibson and John Smoker of BFI Publishing for their expert advice and patience in the production of this book, and the following individuals and organisations for their kind help and co-operation:

Anne Ainsley, Trevor Ainsley, Jim Aitchison, Stephen Archibald, Mick Audsley, David Brown, Judy Cottam, Brian Crumlish, Helen Crummy, Richard Downes, Mamoun Hassan, Mary Holligan, Ian Knox, Jeremy Isaacs, Edwin Lowe, Sue Lowe, Eliza Lynch, Eileen McCallum, Bernard MacKenna, Carolyn MacLean, Hazel McNaught, David Mingay, Alex Norton, Charles Rees, Simon Relph, Yvonne Salmon, Ian Sellar, Jane Sillars, Jon Snow, Robin Soans, Brand Thumin, Dennis Walder, Mary Walder, Cath Wales, Peter West, Roger Wingate, The British Academy, BFI Production, BFI Stills, The Carnegie Trust.

Special thanks to Wilf Stevenson and Colin MacCabe.

John Caughie is Senior Lecturer in Film and Television Studies at the University of Glasgow and co-director of the John Logie Baird Centre. His publications include *Theories of Authorship* and *Television: Ideology and Exchange*, together with a number of articles on television theory and history and on Scottish film culture. He is an editor of *Screen*.

Eddie Dick is Media Education Officer at the Scottish Film Council. He is the editor of *From Limelight to Satellite: A Scottish Film Book*.

Mamoun Hassan is an Independent Film Producer. In 1971 he was appointed Head of Production at the B.F.I. where he initiated the funding of feature films including the Bill Douglas *Trilogy*, Kevin Brownlow's *Winstanley*, Horace Ove's *Pressure*, Peter Smith's *A Private Enterprise*, David Gladwell's *Requiem for a Village* and *Children*, the first part of Terence Davies' Trilogy. He has been Managing Director of the National Film Finance Corporation, a governor of the National Film and Television School and a member of the board of the Scottish Film Production fund. His own productions include the feature film *No Surrender* and two series of *Movie Masterclass*. Among projects he is currently developing is Bill Douglas's script *Justified Sinner*.

Joyce McMillan is Scottish theatre critic for *The Guardian*, and a radio critic of the *Glasgow Herald*; and writes a weekly political/social column for *Scotland on Sunday*. She has written a short history of the Traverse Theatre.

Andrew Noble is a specialist in American and Scottish literature. He has taught since 1966 at the University of Strathclyde where he is now Head of the Literature Section in the Department of English Studies. He has published extensively on Scottish Literature (Robert Burns, R.L. Stevenson, Edwin Muir) and contributed an earlier critical appraisal of Bill Douglas's *Trilogy* to *From Limelight to Satellite*.

Andrew O'Hagan is Assistant Editor at the London Review of Books and has written for the Guardian and the Edinburgh Review. He is currently working on a documentary about child crime for Channel 4.

Duncan Petrie is Research Officer at the British Film Institute. He is the author of *Creativity and Constraint in the British Film Industry* and editor of *Screening Europe* and *New Questions of British Cinema*.

Bill Douglas was – is – the kind of film-maker who has always been rare in Britain. He was not attracted to cinema because he wanted to make a career for himself, or because he wanted to please an audience. He made films from the heart, and from his experience of life. His work, like that of all good artists, was didactic. By which I mean he wanted his audience to know more about life and to understand it better.

I first talked with him many years ago. We met at a coffee bar called 'Act One, Scene One', a friendly meeting place in Soho's Old Compton Street in the good old days. Bill had sent me a script about his childhood, and he wanted advice about how he could make a film of it. Thank God, I immediately understood that he was an artist, and I advised him strongly not to reshape or rewrite his script with the hope of attracting finance. Above all, he should not try to turn it into 'a British film'. Happily, about this time the British Film Institute was starting to back production. Mamoun Hassan became head of the Production Board, and proved himself the kind of patron every artist needs. He and his committee backed Bill Douglas, and so *My Childhood* and *My Ain Folk* and *My Way Home* were made.

Film-making was a kind of agony for Bill because, particularly at the start, his films were torn out of himself. And helping to make his films was a kind of agony for his collaborators too. But there were people around who knew that his talent, his genius were unique. This is how the films were made. After the trilogy, he only managed to make one feature film, and the existence of *Comrades* is miraculous. It would never have been made if Bill had not had the determination, the doggedness, the unreasonableness that every film-maker needs. He worked on further scripts; but of course no one could turn them into the films that he would have made.

Poetry – and these are poetic films – is always a matter of purity and intensity, never of mass. Bill Douglas shot far less footage than many other film-makers. But everything he made showed passionate feeling, as well as a beautifully developing artistry. He was one of the very few. He always will be.

Bill Douglas would have been less than happy at the prospect of a biographical introduction to this book. Naturally modest, in a narcissistic industry, he never sought publicity for its own sake but as a rarely successful means of attracting finance for the purpose of film-making. Added to a chronic anxiety about public exposure is the fact that his career suffered significantly from a simplistic as well as reductive equation of three of his four films with his life. Though his medium involved the most intense realism, Bill was a visionary storyteller, not a factualist. In his creative conception of character as writer and as director he was a perfect exemplar of Blake's dictum that the imaginatively good is achieved by way of minute particulars. Given, then, his own best practice combined with the intensity of my memories of the man, I could not write honestly about him without initially attempting, necessarily brief and comparatively inadequate though it be, to pay the kind of attention to him that, in his art and life, his creative genius brought to others.

> **The question is not at what door of fortune's palace we shall enter in; but what door does she open to us?**
>
> ROBERT BURNS

It is not the least of the paradoxes of Bill's personality that a lifelong desire to remain private was combined, when he felt truly at home, with a charm and warmth unequalled in my experience. Laughter had come belatedly to him in the middle of his abbreviated life; to the joy of his friends he spent his more private hours making up for lost time. His smile was the quintessence of the creative man: it lit up the world for those on whom it was directed.

Bill was born into the depths of the Depression in the mining village of Newcraighall on the outskirts of Edinburgh. The Beveridge (Bill's mother's family) household is still remembered as a home where, almost without exception, only the immediate family had access. Bill's personal and cinematic obsession with doors, then, stemmed from being as a child both closed in and kept out. Such a defensive strategy had not prevented the pain and cruelty of the world gaining access. A Catholic family, the Beveridges had come to Newcraighall in the late 1920s. The father died soon afterwards, to be followed by his son, George, who died, aged nine, from a fall near the railway. Poverty, more than lack of faith, prevented the mother and three daughters participating, like most of the other villagers, in the life of the church in nearby Musselburgh. Certainly the mother's faith was to be tested. Two, some claim three, of her gentle or – in the language of the village – 'saft' girls became pregnant. Poverty and an apparent tendency to withdraw terminally from further hurt combined with inadequate pre-war medical provision and a punitive legalism so that two of the girls were incarcerated for life in state mental asylums. A final Scottish twist to the tale is that the man who made Rose, Bill's mother, pregnant came from Protestant newcomers from the Lanarkshire coalfields, whose entry into the life of the village led to ill-feeling, even violence, with the mainly Irish and Polish inhabitants.

With Granny Beveridge's death, Bill entered the household of his paternal grandmother. Mrs Douglas still, fadingly, exists in the village's memory, with her sharpish clothes, flash jewellery and fondness for drink. For Bill, the most potent memory of her was not the constant emotional rejection of the disgraceful bastard innocently fathered by her divine, fondling son, nor the occasions of hate-filled physical cruelty, but of a woman 'with eyes in the back of her head'. At his most vulnerable, Bill was exposed to a familial near-madhouse where his Granny's sexual frigidity caused her whimsical, cruel and total dominion. On one occasion his Granny hit him so hard with a pot that he feared for his eyesight and subsequently had to get glasses in order to see the blackboard properly. Bill's adult fascination with and adaptation of James Hogg's *Confessions of a Justified*

Bill Douglas (at the apex) as a child at the Newcraighall Pageant, mid-1940s
PHOTOGRAPH COURTESY OF DAVID BROWN

Sinner is entirely comprehensible since, although theologically inarticulate, the practices of the Douglas household conformed to the darkest elements of Scottish Calvinism. Here, principally, we have the division of the will from the flesh in pursuit of power and domination. Here, too, the will becomes the paranoid persecutor of both itself and others in its constant need to police the hidden, usurping enemy of sensuality.

If freedom indoors was impossible, possibilities outdoors for a gifted, self-conscious, stigmatised child were limited: the boys' world of a Scottish mining village, with a brief intermission for improvisation on the football pitch, almost invariably led to the pit, the pub and the betting shop. Bill's 'brother' Ben (actually his cousin), something of a youthful dandy who retains all the spontaneous friendliness of his Beveridge inheritance, adapted to this world. But Bill was never at home in its rough and tumble. His father, 'Black Jock' Douglas, was the worst of role models of Scottish working-class *machismo*. He had inverted Granny Douglas's frigidity into womanising. He was banned from the local dog track for constriction of his whippets' testicles prior to letting them run, victoriously and at the most advantageous odds, in the main event.

Bill is still remembered for improvised theatrical games, with a mainly female cast. Surviving photographs show him to have been the star of the village pageants of the late 40s. Given his temperament, talent and need to escape mentally, the local cinema inevitably became the most important place in his young life.

> For as long as I remember I always liked the pictures. As a boy I spent so much time in cinemas, a friend suggested I take my bed with me. I would have had it been possible. That was my real home, my happiest place when I was lucky enough to be there. Outside, whether in the village or the city, whether I was seven or seventeen, it always seemed to be raining or grey and my heart would sink to despairing depths. I hated reality. Of course I had to go to school – sometimes. And I had to go home and apply myself to the things one has to do. But the next picture, how to get in, was the thing that occupied my mind.
>
> There was never any money to buy a ticket. Still, there were ways. I could get into the Pavilion or The Flea Pit, as we called it, for the price of two jam-jars, washed or unwashed. That they were acceptable unwashed was no mean concession, as I would sometimes have to ferret through buckets for the sticky objects and make a desperate last-minute dash so as not to miss the beginning of the picture.

Sometimes, when I could not find any jars, I had to sneak in by a side-door. What an agonising experience it could be lying in wait, down the side of the cinema, hearing only the sounds of the magic show inside, waiting for what seemed an eternity for that heartening clack of the door opening. Imagine actually penetrating 'the Palace', lurking for a moment inside the toilet so as not to arouse suspicion, sliding open the swing-door to a crack, getting the eyes accustomed to the dark, keeping an eagle watch on the usherette. And then the final brave move forward into the auditorium, careful not to sit on strange laps while searching for a place. It was danger stations if that happened, for at the first signs of a rumpus the torch became a spotlight for interrogation. It was no use saying you had chewed your ticket by mistake. Out you went.

We sat on hard wooden benches, in the 'cheapies'. The Pavilion interior was a cobwebby place: an ancient curtain hung sadly to one side of the screen, sometimes refusing to be drawn, while mice nibbled at the ankles. But who cared about that when Sabu was riding his elephant? It was paradise sitting there in the cosy dark being hypnotised by the play of light. Up there was the best of all possible worlds. To enter this world, that was the dream.

It was some time later that Bill's sole means of escape became the focus for inchoate, adolescent ambition:

Only later did I become aware that real human beings actually worked on the films, that behind the stars was a producer, director, writer, cameraman, designer and so on. It was about this time that I nourished the idea of working in the industry. There was, however, one major snag: how to apply myself. I had no fixed ambition. I would shift from movie star to movie director and back again as the fancy took me. It was all exciting to me.

There was one brief moment of hope when I sent some drawings to Hollywood to a certain Milo Anderson, whose name I picked out of a fan magazine. I waited in suspense for the invitation to become a designer. There was no reply. I can laugh now thinking how imitative my drawings were. So I plodded on, doing any kinds of odd jobs, and they had to be odd because my heart was never in them. In short, I did anything to make enough money to get to the pictures.

About this time – I was seventeen – a certain ritual took place. Returning from my work, I would shave, comb my hair repeatedly, bring my shoes to a high polish and perfect my tie to keep my date – with the cinema. At thirty I was still nowhere near my goal. In fact, it looked as though I was going to preserve my dream forever.

Bill's only marriage was to be to the art of cinema. Though he hardly ever spoke of it, and then either ironically or offhandedly, he had a mysterious sense of his creative path. He seemed to know, intuitively, where to go and how to locate those sadly rare individuals who would open for him the relevant doors of knowledge and opportunity necessary for his growth as creative film-maker.

The first of such meetings came in the somewhat unlikely context of Bill's National Service. The RAF taught Bill to type, and sent him in 1955 to the pre-Suez Canal Zone. After Scotland, the heat and light were in themselves thera-peutic. Egypt also evoked from Bill his first recorded line (little wonder he came to love Chekhov) of that oblique but resonating language so finely present in his screenplays: 'I wonder if you could give me a fill of ink for my pen?' This, what was to prove the most leading of questions, was addressed to Peter Jewell, a deeply cultured film enthusiast from Devon. Peter stimulated in Bill an appetite for music, literature and film, an appetite of which he had been almost entirely unaware. Most important, Peter's knowledge of European art cinema dovetailed with Bill's creative needs. Peter was also the (not always appreciative) audience for Bill's near decade-long litany regarding the allegedly fatal damage of his childhood experience. This, the most important of Bill's friendships, was to last till his death. Peter financed Bill's attendance at the London Film School. He subsequently became his creative sounding-board and, on *Comrades*, his researcher and script editor. In their tiny Soho flat, occupied in 1962 on the very day Larrie Winters (as subsequently filmed in *The Silent Scream*) gunned down a barman in a pub in their street, they put together their extraordinary collection of pre-cinema and cinema artefacts and books. Peter's family were equally open-handed and open-hearted. Barnstaple frequently became home, and was Bill's chosen last resting place. It was also the place of perhaps the most important material gift of his life:

Then an incredible thing happened. A friend gave me an enormous Christ-mas gift. Inside the crate lay all the 8mm equipment any film-maker could wish for. There was a camera, film, projector, editor, splicer, titler – every-thing. I wandered the streets filming everything I could set my eyes on, zooming, tilting, panning, whizzing, rarely static, learning from my mis-takes. In time I became very ambitious. I wrote a screenplay, made costumes, built an adaptation for a Chekhov short story. All amateurs will have the excitement of waiting for the postman to bring back the processed film. Breakfast was the last thing on my mind. I would quickly get up, draw the curtains, and sit there transfixed marvelling at the miracle of everything moving.

Quite unlike the depiction in *My Way Home*, Peter returned from Egypt a year ahead of Bill, who stayed on for the extra money. When Bill did return to Scotland he did not resume his job as a window-dresser with C & A, and subsequently moved to London, contacted Peter, and embarked on a series of odd jobs. Peter was also to provide the key with which Bill opened another important door in his creative growth. Peter had seen Joan Littlewood's company perform at a 1955 Devon festival. He must have transmitted his enthusiasm for the group's radical energies because Bill, following another of his inspired hunches ('It was something that propelled me there'), applied to join her company, Theatre Workshop at Stratford East, in 1959. He was told to report for audition with a prepared piece and also to be ready to improvise. Despite being unsure of what improvisation meant, he succeeded in being enlisted as an unpaid member.

Bill adored Joan Littlewood. She was also the maternal opposite of Granny

In the billet, Egypt 1954

Douglas because, though she also had 'eyes in the back of her head', her intuitive penetration of all around her expressed itself in nurture of individual talent for the greater good of the group. Bill deeply wanted her approval. As an actor she wisely never gave him this. Bill, in a James Deanish phase, was told: 'Forget the psychology.' Her mode of being and her directorial manner were central to the unsentimental education he received from her and which was later put to such significant use:

> I learnt a great deal from her, actually. I learnt about working with actors and how to de-actorise them in a marvellous way, and get them sort of interrelating with each other on a stage, very fast, faster than they knew it was happening. She could also take actors who didn't necessarily under- stand what was going on, and with this amazing ability she could make them believe they had read all of Shakespeare. Astonishing way with people. Such vitality and ... oh, a very big person. So I learnt a lot from there, which I think helped me in a way when I came to work with actors, those that I did work with. I think she was very fond of non-actors herself. She had done one or two productions on the stage where she used people from the street, from the barrows.

Lifelong companion Peter Jewell (Robert in the Trilogy), Egypt 1954

Leaving Joan Littlewood's group in 1960, Bill embarked on a career of acting and writing. Although he subsequently acknowledged himself as a 'terrible' actor of limited range (an inability to laugh on cue suggested the realism of this self-assessment) who intensely disliked being on camera, this side of his life fared much better than that of the writer. The morning post spelled itself out in rejection slips and almost all the 60s scripts, plays, even a novel, are irretrievably lost. He did have a musical, *Solo*, produced in 1962 at Cheltenham, and George Devine at the Royal Court thought highly of a two-act play, *Double Twist*, written in 1963, but it was a shade too black even for that prescriptively dark theatre.

There is a rumoured sighting of Bill as an actor playing a medical student in the first episode of *Dr Finlay's Casebook*. He also appeared as an Ancient Brit in *Carry on Cleo* where, in contrast with Joan Littlewood, Kenneth Williams denied the extras access to the facilities for the stars. More prestigiously, however, he was one of twelve young actors and actresses, including John Thaw, who were

The cast of *The Younger Generation*: L-R (Back Row) Wilfred Downing, Ronald Lacey, Clive Colin-Bowler, Johnny Briggs, Trevor Danby, John Thaw, 'Forbes' Douglas. (Centre) Brian Hewlett. (Front Row) Mary Miller, Mela White, Jill Booty, Gillian Muir, Judy Cornwell, Karal Gardner.
© GRANADA TELEVISION 1961

cast together for Granada's thirteen-part TV series *Younger Generation*, where each was allocated the lead role for one episode. Unfortunately, the tape of Bill's lead role in *Sailor* has not been preserved.

Bill subsequently spoke of spending this period among actors as so valuable in teaching him how to undermine their theatricality when it came to making films. His sense that film-making was what he was born to do took, at long last, a tangible step forward when in 1968, because of his graphic skills and by deleting three years from his age, he was accepted by the London Film School. He graduated in 1969 with first class honours and three student films under his belt. One of these, *Come Dancing*, is a quite extraordinary thirteen-minute piece, filmed at Southend Pier and portraying a homosexual misalliance. One man (to prove another central figure in Bill's life) who responded to *Come Dancing* with the shock inherent in recognising a truly innovative talent was the new Head of Production at the BFI, Mamoun Hassan. Having read the script of *My Childhood*, he screened Bill's student film and immediately committed money to the new project.

With fellow newcomer John Thaw in *The Younger Generation* 1961
© GRANADA TELEVISION 1961

It should be pointed out as an important aside that, although the *Trilogy* is often seen as autobiography, this is too simplistic a response. Certainly many of the events occurred. If one relates Bill's life to the films, however, it soon becomes apparent that he either radically changed chronological sequence or that several key elements did not happen to him at all. For example, he did not have a German prisoner-of-war friend. Bill constantly reiterated Chekhov's maxim that memory was a creative filter employed not for total factual recall but to make art, and that such art, deeply aware of its own formal means, should speak to and for our common condition.

In 1979, with the *Trilogy* completed, Bill was at a particularly low financial ebb. Mamoun Hassan, himself teaching part-time at the National Film and Television School, arranged a post there for Bill. His admiration for Bill as a teacher is only exceeded by his enthusiasm for Bill as film-maker. All who encountered him at Beaconsfield have intense memories of his generous illumination of his subject and of themselves. Colin Young, NFTS Director, wrote:

Bill's former students remember him for one thing above all others and that was the support they got from him. For giving them confidence, for putting them at ease, with their own talent and their own ignorance, and their need to learn. 'When you write,' he would say, 'write only what you see, what you want the audience to see. Nothing more. Every shot is a sentence.' And indeed Bill's scripts were shot lists. 'When writing and directing,' he said, 'it's more important what is left out than what is put in. When you direct, the most important element is stillness. You must create that stillness for the actors so that when they are there, what can happen with them and between them is given a chance to emerge.'

He brought actors out to Beaconsfield. They became part of his gang, above all Kate Scofield and Bill Russell. A common memory for us all of that time is of a group of students in a corner of a stage at Beaconsfield with Bill and Kate, and the look of joy on Bill's face as some small miracle of understanding is developed among them. That joy was bright and searing. It was what after work bound them together and still binds them together. It was almost too bright to look at straight on.

Previous page: On location in Australia during the filming of *Comrades*, 1986
PHOTOGRAPH: ALEX NORTON

When in 1990 Bill joined Strathclyde University's Department of English Studies as Carnegie Visiting Fellow, we got, as a teacher, far more than we bargained for. Apprehensive about vague rumours of a directorial holy terror and fearful of a stringent, austere martinet, we were confronted by a figure emanating creative energy, love of his subject and, not least, laughter.

As a teacher, the only 'no go' area was his future projects. Before they went into production, Bill felt his films should remain inviolate inside his head. He did, however, let me read his scripts for *Confessions*, *Flying Horse* and – a gem-like little comedy he wrote for our students – *The Ring of Truth*. They were generically and stylistically utterly different pieces, and I was astonished by the quality of the writing. I should have known better. A London-based Jock and also one coming (like so many truly great Scottish writers) from 'left-field', Bill tended to disguise the real level of his knowledge and creative intelligence. Like Burns before him, he knew one bitter price of his uncertain advancement was a masking of the self to permit the necessary degree of capricious condescension. A film about Burns was, in fact, on his list of future projects.

While in Glasgow he completed the writing of *Flying Horse*, which Simon Relph at British Screen had commissioned for £15,000. Scottish Television commissioned *The Ring of Truth*, and the pop group, The Fine Young Cannibals, approached him to make a video for their contribution to *Red, Hot and Blue*, a Cole Porter programme financed by Palace Pictures to support Aids charities. None of these projects, for different reasons, got beyond the writing stage. Like other contemporary British film-makers Bill, of course, was a victim of the sycophantically pro-American government's malign fiscal policy towards native cinema. There was a brief chink of light with *Confessions* when it seemed it might go ahead on a reduced budget due to a tempering of the restrictive union practices. When this fell through, Bill wrote to me in June 1990 regarding the death of idealism in cinema and the consequent decline of the industry:

> My only worry – only? – is there won't be any overtime and there goes night shooting. Why can't we work Saturday, for goodness sake? I'm afraid that making money is more important than making movies. There is no mention of minimal crewing – a dozen would suit me instead of sixty but I think the Union was too scared to include this. When they say, 'Basically, I do not believe we necessarily oppose', well, they have no choice with the industry dying at their feet. Where, oh where is the love of doing something for its own sake? They did in Griffith's time. For goodness sake, keep this to yourself or they will hang me.

In fact, his scripts at this time were replete with images of death. *Confessions*, stunningly, opens and closes at a graveside. His pop-videoscript, 'Love for Sale', concludes with an Aids victim stretchered into hospital. *Flying Horse* is about the particular tragedy of Eadweard Muybridge, the pioneer photographer of motion, and the general tragedy of America's betrayal of cinema as communal, revelatory art. *The Ring of Truth* concludes with a surreal funeral at Glasgow's Necropolis, where the mourners are dressed in the now shabby costumes of Hollywood past. As Bill wrote to me from London in June 1990:

> You'll remember I mentioned looking into costumes and props down here. Well, in order to economise I've decided the principals will wear their own clothes or whatever the students and I can find in Oxfam. But the film extras within the film costumes are proving (not unamusingly) a bit difficult. The folk who come to the funeral are all to be dressed as characters from old Hollywood films and I think these might only be found in the big costumiers in London. Amusing, because one is fitting the costumes to the actors, and not the other way round. We will have to find a Scarlett O'Hara with a sixteen-inch waist. Yes, they are to attend the death of the Cinema, but don't ask me who is in the coffin.

Realising the Vision: Bill Douglas directing

PHOTOGRAPH: DAVID APPLEBY

But Bill became more and more fatigued. By early 1991, the cancerous reasons for his exhaustion were belatedly diagnosed by his doctor. For a long time, chain-smoking had been integral to his phenomenal creative concentration. I saw Bill in February of that year, grey, thin, undiagnosed but ambulant. I subsequently saw him in June in Devon days before his death. He handled his last illness with the courage and grace he had brought to his art. He did not want to know it was terminal because he did not want any final doors closed on him. God knows, in this world he had had enough of that.

The last professional portrait: On Musselburgh beach outside Edinburgh, 1990

PHOTOGRAPH: MURDO MacLEOD

The scripts of the *Trilogy* are the centrepiece of this book. They are clearly not substitutes for the films but, in different ways, go beyond mere transcriptions of images. Unusually for writing in script form, they variously remind us of the films, act as commentary on them and stand independently as terse, epigrammatic creations in their own right.

My Childhood was drafted by Bill Douglas for possible publication two years after the film was completed, and that is the version, part novelisation part script, printed here. *My Ain Folk* is the final draft which was the basis of that film's production. *My Way Home* did not exist fully in any draft; the version here was in part reconstructed by Peter Jewell and compiled from a number of sources including, principally, the first draft (the first part of the script printed here), the final draft (the second part) and the dialogue sheets for the whole film.

The Story takes place towards the end of the war.

Scotland. 1945. Sounds of an air raid siren whining. We descend through a shaft of black sky with the noise in our ears. Then gradually the darkness turns to light and the siren dies away. After a moment's silence come softer sounds of breeze and bird song. Suddenly, our downward journey comes to a halt. The first thing we notice is the landscape stretching to the horizon. Then fields. Closer, a deserted mining village.

Closer still, the school. The playground is empty except for the solitary figure of an old woman in black. Age has withered her. She is quite static. She is cold. She is wearing all the clothes she possesses with the exception of her coat which, in her absentmindedness, she has left at home where it also serves as a blanket. She is wearing slippers because she has no shoes. She clutches a black shawl to her head.

Her face has the abstracted look of a mind given to wandering. She has forgotten her reason for coming. She is lost for one brief ecstatic moment in the memory of her own girlhood. But then the children are singing.

The children are gathered together in the assembly hall, hymn books in hand.

> All things bright and beautiful
> All creatures great and small
> All things wise and wonderful
> The Lord God made them all.

The teacher is not singing. She is keeping a look out for drifting heads.

> Each little flower that opens
> Each little bird that sings
> He made their glowing colours
> He made their tiny wings.

At that moment the door opens and in comes the janitor. As quiet as a mouse he relieves himself of his bucket and mop and tip-toes inside. The quickness of his movement suggests urgency.

The janitor approaches the teacher, inclines close to her ear and whispers his message. The teacher nods while casting a glance at one of her pupils.

This is Tommy. He is twelve years old. He appears strangely out of place. His eyes have the seriousness of a person double his age. It is as if the carefree pleasures of childhood had passed him by. Like the others he is poorly dressed, only more so. But he has pride and keeps his head high.

The janitor takes his leave. The teacher progresses amongst her pupils causing some of them to turn with curiosity.

The teacher comes to whisper in Tommy's ear.

My Childhood

The boy goes out of the assembly hall.

> The mountain and the valley
> The river running by
> The sunset and the morning
> That brightens up the sky.

Tommy steps into the playground as weary as an old man. He stands before his grandmother saying nothing. No need to ask questions. He understands. He will take her home where she belongs.

And so these two silent figures make their way through the school gate towards the village.

Their private pain is dwarfed by God's gigantic earth.

> He gave us eyes to see with
> And lips that we might tell
> How great is God Almighty
> Who hath made all things well.

Tommy helps his grandmother up the open stairs. The old woman keeps an anchor hold on the railing. Home is at the top of the landing and that seems a very long way away.

At the top there is a wooden door that looks a thousand years old. Tommy shuts it keeping the world outside.

A fierce wind rages against the mountain of coal dust. It carries us upwards until we can see its crater-like surface.

There is a boy crouched there on his knees. He is grubbing for coal and nearby there is an old newspaper carrying some of his finds. This is Jamie.

On closer inspection we can see he is about nine years old and dirty and that he has worn the elbows of his jumper down so that his shirt peeps through. Jamie is quite lost in his search for coal. No sound of human voices here, no hints of animal life either, just the wind curving and the scrape-scraping of small hands. Then quite suddenly the pit horn moans out like a tired cow. The boy looks up from his chore with more than passing interest. He has every reason to.

Down at the pit shaft gate come the miners weary from their shift.

And from the entrance a rush of children shouting excitedly

> Pit pieces da'
> Pit pieces

This is the circus of their day. There must be something extra tasty about a piece of bread when it has made a long journey into the earth and back.

Jamie moves quickly, snatches up his newspaper package. The headlines hint at news of war.

The boy reaches the edge of the tip just in time to witness the happy moment.

In one joyous surge the children meet with their fathers. There are new imploring cries

> Lift me up da'
> Lift me!

Some get hunch-backs, some fireman's lifts. Others are content to be enclosed in arms. How happy they are.

But not so Jamie. No need for him to go down. He has seen it all before, been there. No lifts for Jamie. Oh well, there is no harm in watching.

So here we have this lonely boy watching the passing of this joyous parade. In a moment the laughter will die away and there will be silence.

Jamie, left there on his own, can only think of one thing. And this thought becomes uppermost in his mind, takes on vast proportions. So much so that he quite forgets his real reason for coming here. He makes off.

He helter skelters down the tip letting the package fall from his grasp. He is too busy thinking about Helmut.

Jamie trying in vain to run away from his bleak childhood

The German POWs can be seen spread out across the field. All is silent except for the clicking sounds of their knives.

Helmut roots a turnip, casting the good vegetable to one side and its waste to the other. He is doing the job without thinking about it. He is thirty. He has an open friendly face. He glances across the field, catches sight of someone and smiles.

Young Jamie is there leaning on the gate.

Helmut goes to join him.

And there they stand with the gate between them. Not a word passes from man or boy but there is an immediate warmth that tells us they are great friends. Helmut winks.

He swings the boy merrily through the air and into the field beside him.

The guard is watching them intently. He looks like the kind of man who has the rule book implanted in his memory, knows how to enforce orders. And there is a suggestion in his eyes that tells us he does not like Germans. Still, he has been known to look the other way.

Helmut wipes Jamie's running nose with his sleeve in a fatherly gesture. Then he crouches low and taps his shoulder. It is his way of telling the boy he is going to give him a lift. Suddenly a voice rackets the silence. It is the guard. 'We're going now!' 'Eine minuten, bitte,' answers Helmut. 'Keine Zeit,' replies the guard. He is saying there is no time.

The workers move wearily towards the tractor wagon.

Jamie settles himself on Helmut's shoulders and 'woosh' in no time at all he is ten foot tall.

They go to join the others in the wagon. The most immediate sound we hear is the clatter of Jamie's tackety boots on the boarding. Finally, they sit down and there is no visible movement at all.

Helmut has his arm round Jamie's shoulders. The boy looks happily content.

Two farm women stroll away across the field giggling at something between themselves.

A group of prisoners have already fallen asleep inside the wagon.

One man stares bored into space.

The guard's rifle lies abandoned against a side flap.

The guard himself is in the field urinating. He seems in no hurry.

The group sleep on, oblivious to the sound of water.

Now the guard turns, whistles his signal and the tractor starts up.

The guard comes to take possession of his rifle. The vehicle pulls away bumping and grinding over lumps of hard earth. We are left with the empty field.

A group of villagers, an old man and two women are standing on the landing of one of the village's open stairs when the tractor makes its entry.

One of the vehicle's large wheels splashes a puddle.

The engine stops. The group on the stairs look on the Germans with a hateful stare.

Helmut swings a reluctant Jamie back to earth and takes back his hat.

Jamie looks numb.

Helmut smiles trying to cheer the boy up.

But the young face looks more miserable than ever.

The tractor pulls away leaving Jamie behind. Helmut waves. 'Auf Wiedersehn, Jamie.' Then he goes leaving a terrible silence.

Jamie feels like crying. He will not see his friend again until tomorrow and that seems a very long way away. Now he must go home. He moves away looking very sorry for himself.

Jamie takes his forlorn Granny by the hand

On the village green a scraggy black cat, a stray, wondering where to go. Now and again he meows to himself for company. Jamie eyes the creature from a secret position behind a row of hanging sheets. He progresses silently until he is quite close to the animal. The cat seems unaware of the prowler. Suddenly, Jamie darts out, his arms outstretched, his voice screeching for all the world like a bomber plane. The frightened creature disappears in a flash.

We are now inside the house. We are close to this door that looks a thousand years old when the latch goes up. Jamie peers inside. He is revealing only one eye and it expresses guilt.

The living room, which is all there is, is so poor, so spare it echoes the smallest sound. Tommy is kneeling on the floorboards busily axeing an old drawer to pieces. He gathers up some of the wood and carries it towards an empty hearth.

The old woman is sitting in a rocking chair. She is perfectly still except for her shivering hands.

Jamie's face is now completely visible. He looks afraid. He feels like running away. But he comes inside.

The wallpaper is so old there are places where it no longer sticks to its surface. Tommy rips off a piece, crunches it up and puts it in the grate.

Jamie is hovering self-consciously beside the bare wooden table. He remembers having stored two pieces of coal in each of his trouser pockets. He fetches out his small offering and puts them on the table top.

The sound of the coals attracts Tommy. He turns to offer Jamie one brief accusatory glance and continues with his chore. Finally, in his own good time, he confronts Jamie.

There is an agonising silence at the table. Jamie, unable to bear the penetration of the accuser's eyes, considers his offering.

Tommy studies the four coals, then the giver. He looks grave.

Jamie decides the best thing to do is not to appear afraid, perhaps even to change the subject. 'I'm hungry.' 'You're selfish!' answers Tommy. And with that he throws himself at Jamie, pulling and pushing, kicking and punching. The boys tumble crazily to the floor.

Their grandmother tries in vain to separate them.

That night a friendly fire burns in the grate. Little flickers of light dart to and fro across the dark room. The family huddle together hypnotised by the flames. The old woman's lips are moving to silent words only she can hear. They are content for a moment. Tommy puts his arm around Jamie's shoulder; all their warring forgotten in the heat.

Much later that night the family lie in bed. They are lying inside what are called bedcupboards. Once they had wooden doors attached that enclosed them inside but Tommy burned them for fuel. Jamie is sharing with his grandmother while neighbouring them lies Tommy. They are wearing all their clothes because there is nothing else to wear.

Jamie draws himself up and leans on his elbow. He appears deep in thought. He looks at his grandmother. 'Granny, where's my ma' and da'?' asks Jamie. But there is no answer. The old woman is fast asleep.

Tommy has been lying awake listening. 'Ma's dead,' he answers.

Jamie is confused. 'What does dead mean?' 'You go up to heaven,' answers Tommy. There is a long silence. 'What's heaven?' Tommy sighs. This is no time for questions. 'My teacher said it's a beautiful house in the sky.' Jamie thinks about that. He understands nothing. 'Go to sleep!' orders Tommy. And silence falls about the room.

Dawn. On the wall just above the old woman's bed there hangs a double portrait in a single frame. We see the faces of two young women, one smiling, the other a little sad. We can hear low sounds of a convoy drifting by. Silence. Then the voice of the old woman. 'Oh, my poor girls'. She is crying quietly to herself. She is lost in the memory of a very private pain. 'What have they done to you?'

A tear lies on the old woman's cheek.

Imprisoned by loneliness: Jamie on the stair landing

Jamie is fast asleep.

Tommy is lying awake. He hears the old woman say 'God curse them'. He understands everything. He will never tell anyone least of all Jamie. But time will unfold the mystery.

A large billowing cloud covers the sun.

Young Jamie is staring up at the sky in absolute wonder.

The cold winter sun stretches itself across the fields eating up hard frost. The boy is still looking up when Helmut comes. He lifts Jamie, swirls him through the air in circles of delight and deposits him inside the truck.

The others are as still as corpses. Helmut and Jamie no sooner take their seats than up goes the rear flap.

The vehicle moves away leaving behind an empty field. The spluttering engine lingers for a while then fades.

Inside the truck Jamie is sharing his ABC book with Helmut. As this will be Helmut's first lesson in English the boy begins at the beginning. 'A is for apple,' says Jamie. 'A is for apple,' answers Helmut with not too much difficulty. 'B is for boy,' says Jamie. 'B is for. . . .' Helmut appears stuck. 'Boy,' repeats Jamie with a lot of emphasis. 'Boy,' answers his friend in a very German way. 'C is for Cat.' 'C is for Cat,' repeats Helmut. He is doing well. Jamie is delighted.

The truck travels merrily up a sloping field.

The boy continues his lesson. 'Dooog' answers Helmut, a little unsure. 'Dog,' repeats Jamie. 'Dog,' answers Helmut again. 'Good,' says Jamie. And he smiles.

The vehicle thunders into the village and stops.

Helmut flits a miserable Jamie back to earth. Then he hands down the ABC book. The boy shakes his head. 'No, it's for you, Helmut.' The man seems to understand this simple gesture. He thanks Jamie and asks in German if he is going home to his mother. Jamie does not really understand but he nods just the same. 'Auf Wiedersehn,' says Helmut clutching the gift. The boy waves trying to keep up his spirits. In a moment the truck will go away and he will be a little figure left behind.

A young POW goes towards the farmhouse to collect his dinner.

The farmer's wife arrives promptly with the food.

She places in the hands of the young German an enamelled basin piled high with mashed potato.

He carries the meal away.

He goes to lean on the truck where a friend is waiting. The rest of the soldiers are spread out across the grass preoccupied with the business of eating. Helmut remains quite separate. He is sitting on an old oil drum perusing his book.

Over at the truck the young German nudges his friend to look.

Helmut is completely lost in his newly acquired ABC, and has forgotten his food.

The two Germans chuckle to each other.

A blustering day in the village graveyard. Tommy is looking down at his mother's grave. The headstone is overgrown with weeds. There is complete disillusion on his young face. A crow squawks hauntingly in the silence.

A fresh bunch of poppies adorns a grave nearby. Tommy steals them.

The boy strolls down the village street with the flowers in his hand. He is going to make a present of them to his grandmother to cheer her up. Some distance ahead of him comes a man with a dog, a whippet on a lead. The man has a round face and his name is Mr Knox. Mr Knox is completely absorbed in himself. The man and the boy pass one another without a word or a glance.

Barely a moment later Tommy turns to give his full attention to the man.

Mr Knox reaches the top of the street. Ahead of him there are two neighbouring houses. The house on the left has a window with eight panes of glass, the one on the right, two panes, both equal size just different in design. Outside the house with two panes stands a woman of advanced age. This is Mrs Knox. Mr Knox advances towards his mother.

The woman nudges her son to look. At closer inspection she has a face like a hawk. Mr Knox turns as directed and for some reason he looks a trifle uneasy.

There is an expression of hate on Tommy's face. He spits on the ground in order to make his feelings more felt. Then he departs.

The poppies are withered now. They hang limp from a tea cup.

The flowers are made insignificant by the table top and, in turn, the table by the room. The latch clacks up on the living room door. Jamie comes in carrying a kettle which he places on the table.

The boy has need of the tea cup and so he sploshes the dead poppies on to the floor. That done, he proceeds to fill the cup with boiling water. Up and up the water goes until it overflows on to the table. Now he empties the cup itself.

Jamie goes to kneel before his grandmother. He places the warm cup inside her hands.

He encloses her hands in his for extra warmth and pats them gently.

One day there is a strange bicycle at the foot of the stairs. There is a moment's silence, then the sound of the door closing.

Inside the old woman looks agitated. From somewhere in the room comes the voice of a man. 'How are you, old one?' asks the visitor, kindly. 'Getting along all right, are you?' The old woman does not answer.

Jamie and Tommy are standing behind their grandmother's chair. They feel safer there. They have never set eyes on the man before.

Mr Brown is nearing forty. He holds a birdcage in his hand. He looks more and more uncomfortable. He fetches the canary into sunlight on the table.

The boys are fascinated by the small yellow creature. But they remain where they are, hiding their feelings.

The canary flutters to and fro inside its cage whistling a happy tune.

'It's for your birthday, son. Like birds, do you?' asks Mr Brown.

Jamie glances up at Tommy. He is not sure to whom the visitor is referring.

'Come on then, son,' encourages Mr Brown. 'Not frightened of me, are you?'

Tommy, feeling the man must be talking to him, releases himself from his grandmother's grasp.

He goes towards the visitor. He plays for a moment with the canary.

Jamie is feeling very sorry for himself. He hides his face inside his grandmother's shoulder. The old woman comforts the jealous boy.

'Is it really my birthday?' asks Tommy, shyly. The man smiles warmly. 'Did you not know that? A big laddie like you?' He ruffles the boy's hair affectionately. At that moment Tommy feels instinctively the man before him must be his father. But he is too frightened to ask. Mr Brown's eyes have a long-lost look in them. They suggest a hint of private pain, regret, an infinite sadness. 'What are you going to be when you grow up, son?'

Suddenly, the old woman explodes with energy. It is as if she has been given a new lease of life. 'I hope he won't be anything like you. Now get out!' Mr Brown is nervous. 'I brought him a birthday present because I was thinking about him.' But the old woman is thoroughly at war. 'He is not needing anything from the likes of you. Go on, get out!'

'Right!' says Mr Brown, thus fetching the argument to a close. He turns to go. On his way out he glances briefly at the photograph of his wife.

The young woman appears not to be smiling now, but laughing at him.

Previous page: Tommy in ecstasy on the railway bridge

Mr Brown pulls the door behind him. Young Tommy looks disconsolate. 'What did you do that for?'

'Because he's no earthly good to man or beast,' answers his grandmother. Jamie smiles with satisfaction.

Tommy bolts out of the house. There is no time to lose.

He reaches the landing, shouts, 'Da?'

Down in the street Mr Brown is already on his bicycle.

The boy scrambles down the stairs as fast as his legs will carry him.

He hurries breathlessly after the bicycle. 'Da, come back. Da, come back!' But his father does not respond.

Mr Brown journeys alone down a country lane. His anger causes the machine to shake. He turns a corner and disappears.

Tommy is beside himself with grief. He is crouched in a corner beside some railway sleepers. This is where he comes when he wants to be on his own.

That night the old woman is standing on the stair landing waiting for the boy to come back. A lonely dog howls in the silence.

The howl spreads across the dark landscape and dies.

In the very early hours of the morning Jamie hangs the birdcage up in the window. He is hoping to attract Tommy.

A little later the boy returns, though not immediately to the house. He goes to sit on an opposite step.

The canary comes to life behind the window, flits back and forth. It too must be wanting him to come back.

Tommy looks up at his pet. His eyes are tired and his face is very dirty. But for all that, he appears happy to see his canary. Then, quite suddenly, the boy's expression turns to horror. He is wondering if he is seeing things.

Behind the widow – there are no curtains, so there is a clear view – there is a hint of disturbance The old woman has a broom in her hand and she is trying to dislodge the cage. She has no trouble and boom down it comes with a crash.

The boy springs up.

He races upstairs.

He bursts into the room. There is a terrible noise inside. The old woman is bashing the cage with her broom. Tommy wrenches the weapon free, rescues his birthday present and puts it on the table. Then he turns to his grandmother and says angrily,

'Just you leave my birdcage alone. I'll give it away if you want but just leave it alone.' He pauses a moment so that she might understand. 'Okay?' He picks up his gift and leaves the house. The old woman sobs like a little child.

The boy descends the stairs, panting. In the well of the staircase there is a coal cellar. He disappears inside and slams the door shut.

Tommy huddles in the darkness with the birdcage on his lap. The canary is perfectly still but unharmed. The boy prods the cage trying to encourage his pet to flutter happily again. 'Joey, what's wrong?' The bird remains silent. 'Never mind. I'll look after you,' says Tommy. Then they remain content with each other's company.

Jamie approaches the coal cellar door, tries to open it. 'Go away!' snarls Tommy, holding the door fast. 'Tommy, Granny's lost,' says Jamie. He means she has wandered away. And he is worried because being old she has been known not to remember her way back home. 'I'm not bothered,' shouts Tommy. Jamie turns away. He is busily wondering what to do when he hears a cat meowing.

It is the same scraggy black stray. The animal senses Jamie's presence and runs off. It reaches the edge of the pavement and ponders the best way to go.

Jamie is hypnotised by the creature. He decides to have the animal for a pet.

The stray charges off.

Jamie in hot pursuit.

The old woman is standing in grass that reaches to her waist. She is perfectly lost.

Jamie hurries towards his grandmother with the protesting animal firmly locked under his arm. He takes the forlorn woman by the hand and gently leads her away.

A Spitfire haunts the sky.

Jamie is now sitting on the stair landing. His hand shields his eyes while he watches the plane.

The Spitfire drones deep into the sky and disappears. Out of the silence comes the sound of heavy footsteps.

Jamie turns his attention to the street below.

Mr Knox, the man who keeps the whippet, is there looking up. He beckons Jamie forward.

The boy descends with caution. He reaches the end of the railing then holds back shyly. There is no reason to, the man looks friendly enough. Jamie finally comes forward and as he does so Mr Knox stoops to his level.

The man smiles warmly.

Jamie looks puzzled. He has never seen the man before.

Mr Knox holds forth a shining sixpenny piece between two fingers.

The coin tantalises Jamie. He completely forgets the man, grabs the money and bolts upstairs.

Mr Knox looks a little disappointed by their short encounter. Perhaps he wanted to talk.

Jamie remains watching from the safety of the landing.

The man goes away through an alley. There is something very lonely about him.

Jamie and his friend, Helmut, are huddled together on a grassy slope. Now it is Helmut's turn to teach his young pupil a lesson in German. 'Das ist mein Buch, Jamie,' says Helmut holding the ABC book open. The boy listens intently. The man turns a page. 'Apfel.' 'Apfel,' echoes Jamie without the slightest difficulty. 'Katte,' continues the German. 'Katte,' repeats Jamie. He is surprised how similar the words sound in a foreign language. But Helmut, always ready for fun, has a surprise in store for his young friend. The next thing he says is very long and complicated. Jamie leaps up on to his knees, protesting. 'I want something easy.' Helmut laughs. He throws himself back on to the grass and pulls Jamie towards him. 'Auf Wiedersehn, Jamie,' says Helmut. And before the startled boy knows what is happening, he and his friend are toppling head over heels, merrily down to the bottom of the hill.

A makeshift cover hangs over Tommy's bedcupboard. The boy is hiding inside in the company of his canary. The bird chirps sweetly.

The old woman is fast asleep in her rocking chair. Jamie is sitting by the table with the scraggy black cat on his knee. Clearly the creature does not want to play and with an angry snarl it leaps on to the floor. Jamie folds his arms. He looks bored. He comes to his grandmother and touches her cheek but the old woman shows no reaction. Jamie moves quietly away.

He comes to sneak a peep at the canary. Tommy's head appears instantly through a hole in the cover. 'Get away,' he orders. This is too much for Jamie to bear. 'If you don't let me play I'll tell granny you've got the canary,' says the disappointed boy. 'You're just jealous because it was my da' who gave it to me.' Jamie looks very hurt. 'He's my da' too.' 'No he's not,' charges Tommy. He worries for a moment in case Jamie is going to cry. That would surely put an end to the canary. 'I know a secret,' offers Tommy. 'What?' asks Jamie. Tommy draws close to the other's ear.

Their grandmother remains asleep.

The whispering is over. 'Well?' asks Jamie. 'Okay,' answers Tommy. He slides off his bed.

He accompanies Jamie towards the door. He pauses briefly to whisper in Jamie's ear. 'He's got a whippet.' 'A whippet?' exclaims Jamie. 'Sssh.' The old woman wakes up. She looks angry. The boys leave the house.

Once in the street, Tommy points a finger. 'Jamie, your da' lives over there.' He is indicating the window with two panes. But they are a little distance away from the place in question and Jamie is unsure. 'Where?' he asks. 'There,' says Tommy. Only now he has had second thoughts. Perhaps he is afraid of his grandmother for his hand drifts to the neighbouring window with eight panes.

And so Jamie comes to this house in search of his father. He knocks on the door but there is no answer. He goes to tap on the window but still no answer.

Tommy is sitting at the bottom of the stairs feeling very sorry for himself. It appears he and his grandmother have had more than words.

Jamie is standing some distance away tugging aimlessly at a loose chain on a coal cellar door. He is looking equally sorry for himself.

Tommy glances up still nursing a sore ear. 'Get away,' he says angrily.

Jamie gives a wounded look at his aggressor.

'Get away. I got hit because of you,' adds Tommy.

Jamie goes away.

Visiting Jamie's mother in hospital

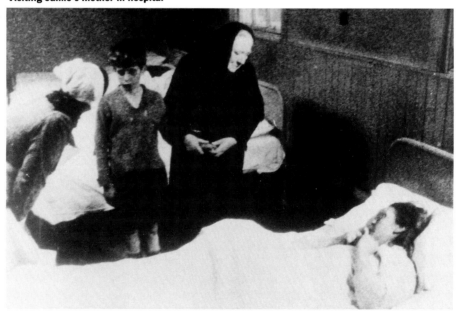

A group of old men are keeping themselves company in the village street. They are laughing and talking amongst themselves.

Jamie is watching them through a stair railing. But he can hear nothing. He is far too lost inside himself thinking about his father.

The old men drift across the square in silence.

Jamie continues watching them. They are like figures in a dream.

Finally, the group disappear round a corner leaving the place deserted.

The field is a happier place because Helmut is there. The man is sitting on a wall eating bread.

Jamie is crouched on the soft earth sharing the same food.

They are both perfectly quiet, perfectly content to be in each other's company. The boy finishes eating. He sneaks up behind Helmut who pretends not to notice. The boy throws his arms round the man's neck and hugs him tight. 'I love you, Helmut,' whispers Jamie. Helmut smiles. He understands perfectly.

That night there is an air raid in the area surrounding the village. We hear the drone of planes then sounds of bombs booming on the horizon. From inside the air raid shelter comes the voice of an old man singing.

> Oh! Rowan tree. Oh! Rowan tree.
> Thou'lt aye be dear to me
> Entwin'd thou art wi many ties
> O hame and infancy.

The two boys and their grandmother huddle together inside. Tommy is fast asleep.

The face of the old man radiates happiness. His song is about the home of his youth.

> Thy leaves were aye the first o spring
> Thy flow'rs the summer's pride
> There wasna sic a bonny tree
> In a the countryside.
> Oh! Rowan tree.

Jamie turns away from his grandmother.

On a bunk nearby there is a little girl. She is fast asleep and next to her, close to her open hand, is a rosy apple.

Jamie sneaks a look at his grandmother to make sure she is not watching him.

The apple is tantalising.

Jamie, unable to bear it any longer, stretches out his hand. Nearer and nearer the fruit he goes. He is about to pick up the apple when suddenly his grandmother pulls him back. She shakes a finger angrily. A long wailing cry sounds the All Clear.

The sound explodes into the cold light of the morning. Drowsy figures emerge on to the green going their own separate ways.

The sound follows Tommy and his grandmother into the house. Then it dies. Jamie's tackety boots clatter up the stairs.

Jamie slams the door shut.

Tommy's face is contorted in silent agony.

The old woman stares dumbfounded.

The birdcage lies abandoned on the floor.

The scraggy black cat is eating the canary's innards. Tommy's hand jerks the creature up by the scruff of the neck. Jamie springs forward to rescue his pet. 'Give me back my cat!' screams Jamie. 'He was hungry.' The poor animal, finding itself pulled to and fro, snarls and spits.

The old woman is too tired to separate them.

Tommy thrusts Jamie away. 'I'm going to kill it!' He drags the cat across the room.

Jamie looks numb. We can hear the swing of Tommy's arm and a dull thump as the cat reaches a wall.

On the stair landing Tommy has the dead creature by the tail. He throws it over the railing.

The animal lands in the gutter.

Tommy slides down the stair railing, scampers off through an alley.

A steam train trailing coal wagons crashes forward.

Tommy hoists himself above the fence of sleepers.

The train gathers speed.

Tommy lowers himself into a pathway.

The engine chugs and sways. Steam billows from its funnel.

Tommy races behind the sleepers, legs and arms crazily flying.

Mountains of steam.

Faster legs, faster arms.

Tommy dives towards the bridge.

He bursts on to the bridge landing. And within seconds he is lost in steam. It is as if he had ascended to the clouds. He spreads out his arms like a bird in flight. His face is ecstatic. He remains there long after the steam has dispersed, too thrilled to break this magic spell.

Jamie sneaks a look round a corner in the village.

Ahead of him Mr Knox is walking his whippet. He is progressing towards the house which has the window with eight small panes. Jamie watches this man who once gave him sixpence whom he now thinks must be his father.

The boy decides to follow.

Mr Knox pauses for a moment to pat his dog. On his left is the window with eight panes and on his right the house which has the window with only two panes. When Mr Knox moves again he veers right. He snaps the door shut behind him. Jamie comes to hover around outside.

Mrs Knox is watching Jamie from behind her window curtain. The boy, sensing her gaze, looks uncomfortable. Mrs Knox utters the word 'sixpence' with a touch of irony and moves away.

Mr Knox looks uncomfortable. He had been aware of the boy following him. He was hoping the boy would give up, go away, because he did not want his mother to notice. Now he had had to admit the incident of the sixpence. Mrs Knox was not happy. She preferred to keep the past forgotten. She wanted her son to stay with her. Mrs Knox comes to her son where he is sitting by the fireside. She smoothes him as one would a child.

She remembers a time when he was a child just like Jamie. He had been an orphan and she had brought him up as her own son. She loved him, possessed him. 'You're mine,' says Mrs Knox. 'I took you in and cared for you when nobody in the world cared. God in heaven, the dreams I had for you.' She thinks about Jamie's mother. 'She was a whore, son.'

Jamie remains outside looking more and more unwanted. Mrs Knox continues, 'All women are whores.'

Mrs Knox smiles affectionately at her son. 'You're a King,' she says, embracing him. 'How can they know?' Mr Knox resigns himself.

Jamie waits for a long while, then he gives up.

Jamie is looking through a bus window. The engine throttles, gathering speed.

Helmut is in a field. He becomes a small figure drifting away.

Jamie watches after his friend with a numb face.

Then Helmut is gone and there is just emptiness.

Jamie is sitting beside his grandmother when the bus conductress approaches. 'Where to?' she asks. The old woman has no money. She pretends not to hear. The conductress sighs. The boy unpins a letter from inside his grandmother's coat and hands it to the young woman. She scans the letter with an even deeper sigh. She is too busy to care. 'That will be one and three.' She hands Jamie back the paper. Jamie searches for money inside his grandmother's pocket. The conductress stares through the window, gathering impatience. Jamie fetches out a rosy apple. He is mesmerised. The bus conductress runs off two tickets. Her manner is gruff but she understands. 'Never mind, we'll pay for it.' She goes.

Jamie looks at his grandmother. He is thinking it is the same apple from the air raid shelter. The old woman senses what is in the boy's mind. She says nothing, just smiles and winks.

The bus continues its journey.

The old woman is fast asleep, lulled by the bus' rhythmic sway. Jamie is reading the letter. He looks puzzled. 'Granny, who's Mary?' Getting no answer, he goes back to his letter. He turns to his grandmother once more. 'Granny, I don't want to go to a hospital.'

The hospital has an appearance more like an ancestral home. In front of its colonnades there is a spacious lawn trimmed with flower beds.

Inside, the first sound we hear is a nurse's clapping hands. Her voice is bright and breezy. 'Come on, Mary.' In a bed, in the raw summer light of sun on frosted glass, lies a figure completely hidden under covers. Then we see fists clutching the covers fast. The nurse tugs at the covers but they won't give.

Jamie and his grandmother are standing quite close to the bed. The nurse wrenches off the covers. 'Now, Mary, this is no way to behave when you've got visitors, is it?' She might be speaking to a child. 'No, it isn't.'

The nurse turns to smile at Jamie. We notice she has healthy apple-blossom cheeks.

Jamie, feeling a little shy, does not return the smile. His grandmother puts the apple in his hand and nudges him forward.

The fruit is placed on the bed.

Jamie returns to his grandmother's side. The nurse tucks in the bedcovers while taking notice of the apple. She proceeds to tend her patient, combs her hair. 'We've got to make you look pretty, haven't we?' She pats the pillow. 'Yes, we have.' She progresses towards the apple, patting and tucking the covers as she goes. 'There, there, that's better. Now we're all nice and comfy.' In a flash the nurse pockets the apple. She finishes her chores, then approaches Jamie. The boy is horrified. The nurse smiles warmly as if nothing unusual had taken place. 'And what's your name?'

'Jamie,' says the boy. 'You stole my apple.' But the nurse pretends not to hear. 'Jamie, that's a very nice name. Would you like to say hello to your mother, Jamie?'

The nurse ushers the boy towards the bed. Then she withdraws in a hurry, tapping her pocket like a schoolgirl with a choice sweet.

Jamie's face is numb. He understands nothing.

His mother stares abstractedly into space. Her face is ghost-white from lack of fresh air.

The old woman cries tears of anguish.

Jamie turns to look at his grandmother. He feels miserable. He returns to his mother. But it is too late. She has hidden her face beneath the covers again.

That night the old woman and Jamie come to the house of the boy's father. She spits on the doorstep, releasing feelings of hate.

One bleak day the old woman is stranded in a field. She moves in circle upon circle not knowing who she is or where she is going.

She wails like a wounded animal. She sways to and fro cradling a grubby newspaper parcel.

The boys comfort their grieving Grandmother

Tommy and Jamie hurry down the field as fast as their legs can carry them. Tommy comes to a halt. He looks worried.

The old woman shows no signs of recognition.

Tommy comes to his grandmother's side.

Jamie stands a short distance away.

Tommy takes the parcel from the old woman and studies its contents. He looks horrified by what he sees. He throws the parcel to the ground.

A dead bird clings to the newspaper.

Jamie looks sadly at the old woman.

Tommy embraces his grandmother, holds her tight. Then he takes her by the hand and leads her away.

Night. The war has ended. There is a huge bonfire on the village green. Crowds surround the flames, rejoicing.

In the morning smouldering ashes and silence.

There is a bus waiting at the edge of the field. The POWs are inside.

A blustering day. Helmut and Jamie are seen high on a hill preparing to fly a kite.

A colourful kite dancing in the sky.

Jamie and his friend descend into a ditch. Helmut is wearing civilian clothes. He passes the string to Jamie. 'Nice kite,' says Helmut. 'For you, Jamie.' Jamie expresses delight.

The kite flaps merrily in the air, then it takes a giant swoop. The guard's voice is heard shouting. 'We're going now!'

Helmut glances across the field. He must go now. 'Auf Wiedersehn, Jamie,' says Helmut. He hurries away. Jamie is distraught. He is so stunned by Helmut's departure he lets the kite go.

The kite falls from the sky.

Jamie tears across the field trying to keep up with the bus. 'Helmut!' he screams. 'Helmut!' The sound spreads across the landscape and dies and nobody hears but himself.

Jamie is beside himself with grief. He is crouched in a corner beside some railway sleepers. This is where he comes when he wants to be on his own.

Jamie lies in bed feeling sorry for himself. His hand covers his face. Tommy comes to sit beside him. 'What's wrong, Jamie, aren't you feeling well?' Jamie does not answer. 'Is it because of your da?' Silence. 'Never mind, granny and me will look after you.'

Jamie is inconsolable. He knows nothing in the world will bring Helmut back. He draws a cover over his face.

One cold winter's day, Jamie is sitting at the table. Tommy comes into the room carrying a bottle containing some milk. On the table there is a cooking pot, two bowls and a lump of bread.

Tommy divides the bread between the three. He soaks one of the bowls of bread with milk and passes it to Jamie. He lifts the second bowl for his grandmother.

Jamie eats in silence using his fingers. A little while later it occurs to him that there is not another sound in the room. He looks across at his grandmother. He moves away from the table.

He comes to stand beside Tommy, who is still holding the bowl of food in his hand.

Jamie picks up his grandmother's hand.

There is no response, so he lowers her hand back to her lap.

The old woman's head is tilted back in the chair. Her mouth hangs open, static. She is dead.

All alone in the world: finding Granny dead

The two boys stare at their grandmother as if they could not believe this could happen. 'I'd better go and fetch your da,' says Tommy mournfully. He puts the food back on the table and leaves the house. Jamie continues to look at the lifeless figure, then, unable to bear it any longer, he runs away.

He runs towards the railway bridge.

He emerges on to the railway lines through a gap in the sleepers.

He presses his ear to the line listening for a train. Everywhere is silent.

The boy crouches by the sleepers and cries. From the distance comes the sound of a train. Jamie hears it, looks up.

Steam billowing from the engine's funnel.

Jamie hurries on to the bridge landing as the train bursts underneath.

The boy climbs over the bridge rail, steadies himself, and jumps through the steam.

Jamie is lying on his back in a coal wagon. He struggles himself up to a crouched position.

The village recedes.

Jamie spits at this place that has caused him so much pain.

The village disappears.

The wagons drift away all sound and sway towards the horizon.

A beautiful Scottish landscape full of sun and laughter and lilting music.

But it is all happening on a screen in a drab picture house.

Young Tommy is crying in the darkness.

Beyond the cinema foyer we see a heartless place. We enter into its cold deserted streets and the houses and the bleak sky that falls like a sheet behind the pit wheel.

Below at the pit shaft gate we see a group of miners, waiting, static, like images out of a dream. They drift silently away inside the gate mouth.

Beyond the shaft gate we see a square of white sky. Suddenly, the lift descends, black earth rushing up to shut out the light. We hear the sound of a long unbroken mountainous whine.

MY AIN FOLK

A Scottish Mining Village. Peacetime 1946.

Black. The whining sound cuts abruptly.

Now we see in the cold light of day an open stairway in the village. At the bottom of the steps there is Jamie's father, Mr Knox, in his pit clothes, agitated, pacing up and down. And at the top, on the stair landing, there is a man in black waiting.

Mr Knox kicks a stone to release his anger.

Young Tommy peering through a hole in the foyer curtain. He is eyeing a cash desk inside which there is a snoozing cashier. Somewhere below her domain there is a 'Today' poster heralding *Lassie Come Home*. And above, a sign reading 'Admission 5d or Two Jam Jars'.

A collection of the sticky jam jars isolated.

Tommy's hand drawing back the curtain.

Mr Knox is down in the street. He has his back to us. He comes to a halt.

Close, in the distance beyond the man, waits his mother, Mrs Knox.

Mr Knox looks defeated.

MRS KNOX Finish!

Mr Knox turns to make that gesture with his hand.

And the man in black disappears from the landing.

We see an old woman's dead face before the coffin lid covers her.

Young Jamie curled up inside a rocking chair with his face buried in his arms.

Back in the street.

MR KNOX You're too late!

Mr Knox and Tommy are facing one another. The boy has a look of defiance on his face.

Mr Knox waits for an excuse. He appears calm.

MR KNOX Well?

The boy echoes the man.

TOMMY Well?

Tommy has his hands inside the jam jars like boxing gloves. He has adopted a couldn't-care-less attitude. He clonks the jars head on to emphasise his point. He makes to by-pass the man on his way upstairs. Mr Knox stops him short. The boy struggles, curses. Mr Knox slaps the boy hard on the face.

The slap exploding about them in the street.

A shower of grit clattering on the coffin.

Mrs Knox is peering round the corner of her window blind. There is the sound of a passing vehicle descending in volume. She lets her blind go.

A stationary black van at the foot of the open stairs.

Inside the room all hell is let loose. Jamie is screaming and struggling to get free. His neck is hooked by a uniformed arm.

And Tommy is trying to fight off a pair of arms clamping his waist.

The boys are in the grip of two uniformed charity workers who are trying to get them out of the house. One of the men says reasonably, 'We're going to look after you', in answer to which Tommy yells

TOMMY We can look after ourselves!

Tommy kicks violently at the legs of the man holding Jamie. The pained man grabs up the offender's foot and Jamie makes a dash for it under the table.

TOMMY Run for it, Jamie, run for it. I'll find you.

Jamie flies out the door

And across the landing

And up the street shouting an agonised

JAMIE Da!

Mr Knox sitting by the fire. Across from him, Mrs Knox at the window, unmoved.

Jamie runs to the door and knocks.

The van is coming up the street.

Mrs Knox opens the door. Jamie cries

JAMIE They're going to take me away!

He squeezes himself behind her skirts.

The boy dashes across the firelit living room like an alarmed rabbit. Mr Knox has disappeared from his fireside chair. Jamie dashes through a bedroom door.

Outside, moving in the breeze, a streamer reading 'Welcome Home Son'.

Above Mrs Knox's head, suspended round the doorway, linked to the streamer, hang limp decorations and flags. The car arrives, first obliterating the woman then revealing her as it shrieks to a halt.

Close, Mrs Knox looking amiable.

The picture of sadness: Jamie goes to live with his other Granny

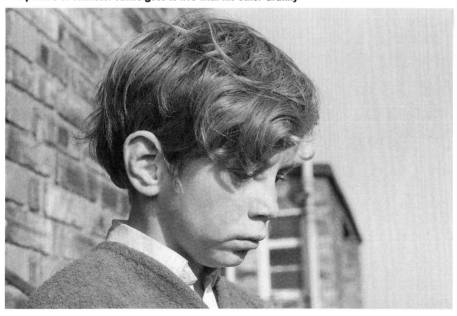

Jagged antler horns on the bedroom wall.

Jamie, a snared figure crouched in a corner of this room.

Closer, Jamie, head cradled in his arms, hearing muffled conversation. Then a more immediate sound of breathing reaches him and he peeps up, sees

John, who is Mrs Knox's other son. He is sleeping inside a bedcupboard. Close beside him there is a chair, and there, draped over the chair back, there is a soldier's uniform with decorations for bravery on the breast.

Suddenly, the door opens with a clack.

Jamie startles.

Mrs Knox's hand is seen on the door latch. We hear

CHARITY WORKER By law the father will have to take full responsibility for the child's welfare.

MRS KNOX He was always welcome here!

A whippet paddies into the room and the door closes.

In the firelit room Mrs Knox says

MRS KNOX My son's character is impeccable, beyond reproach!

But Mr Knox is hiding inside the lavatory.

Mr Knox's hand flicks nervously on the whippet's chain lead.

The whippet stares at Jamie.

And Jamie stares back at the whippet.

Tommy's numb face behind the van's rear window.

The van going away along a country road.

Jamie is standing in a corner by the living room door looking unsure of himself.

Mrs Knox is sitting by the fire. She has her back to us. She is invisible except for her head above the chair and her elbow on the arm rest. Mr Knox comes from the bedroom putting on his jacket. He comes to kiss his mother. They share a brief silent conversation of the eyes. Then Mr Knox whistles for the dog and it follows him.

Mr Knox goes out of the door, attaching the animal to its lead. He goes without looking at Jamie. It is as if the boy did not exist. Jamie feels unwanted. He hears the outer door slam shut.

MRS KNOX Your mother ruined my son's life!

Jamie is confused. He is wishing he had let them take him away.

Mrs Knox is quite calm but there is a note of irretrievable loss in her voice.

MRS KNOX He had the makings of a great man.

At that moment John comes out of the bedroom in his shirt tail. He glances briefly at his mother before moving away.

MRS KNOX He could have had the whole wide world at his feet.

John is now at the open living room door. Behind him we can see Mrs Knox. Her words come as light as a dwindling feather.

MRS KNOX All gone!

John pushes the door further to reveal Jamie. He nods his head back to connect with his mother, then he winks at Jamie. During the wink Mrs Knox swings round, for nothing escapes her. John moves quickly away, shutting his mother out then revealing her. She slams her fist down on the chair arm.

The weight of this fist.

Her sudden angry face.

MRS KNOX She wanted to destroy him!

A very frightened Jamie.

Mrs Knox falls silent. During the silence there is heard the sound of the toilet flushing. Then silence.

MRS KNOX What made you think you had the right to come here?

Jamie goes quietly away closing the door behind him.

Jamie running along the pavement and up the open stairs towards the landing.

He slams the door shut behind him.

A delicate butterfly inside an airless jam jar.

Jamie lying on the bed with his face buried in a pillow.

Jamie on the landing, hands cupped to mouth, making a long forlorn cry into the night.

JAMIE Tommy!

The cry embraces the landscape and dies.

A sunny glen full of trees and water.

Jamie's clothes burning on dead leaves.

The boy sitting in a stream having his head washed by his father.

Mr Knox sauntering towards us along a narrow country road. Jamie is coming some distance behind with a damp towel rolled up under his arm. The scrubbed boy is wearing cleaner but similar clothing to his old clothes. Mr Knox turns to wait for his son to catch up. Jamie comes for a bit then, seeing his father facing him, stops as wary as a rabbit for a snare.

Mr Knox looks friendly enough.

MR KNOX How old will you be now, son?

Jamie looks moodily at the ground. He hears his father say

MR KNOX Mmm?

And frowns in answer.

Mr Knox looks like a man who knows he has failed as a father and turning back now is almost impossible. But he makes a final bid.

MR KNOX Would you like to come and live with me?

Jamie shakes his head firmly. Then he bolts away.

He hurries past the man. Mr Knox doesn't bother to turn to watch the boy go.

Jamie is again standing in the corner by the living room door and completely unsure of himself.

Mrs Knox is sitting in her chair with her back to him. Her hands are clasped together in her lap. The room is perfectly silent. And there is no movement except for the woman's thumbs circling each other in an endless clockwise movement. Suddenly they stop.

Jamie watches.

Now the thumbs make a reverse movement. Then they part. The hands turn into fists. The body looms up. Nervousness in the air.

She charges across the room, pulls open a drawer, brings out a knife.

Jamie runs for his life.

The frightened boy runs out of the house followed closely by a mad Mrs Knox. But she doesn't pursue Jamie. Instead she makes for the house immediately next door. She bangs her fist on the door.

Jamie's shivering face in a corner.

The woman now batters on the window pane but gets no answer.

Classroom. A group of children behind desks. They are singing. Jamie singing with them is finally isolated.

> Summer suns are glowing
> Over land and sea
> Happy light is flowing
> Bountiful and free
> Everything rejoices
> In the mellow rain
> Earth's one thousand voices
> Join the sweet refrain

Jamie has wet the floor.

All the children, rear view.

> All good gifts around us
> Are sent from heaven above
> So thank the Lord
> Oh thank the Lord
> For all his love

And as the singing continues we see what will become of the children.

We are in the cage, inside the pit shaft gate. Once more we are leaving behind the good light and once more the black earth is rushing up to shut it out.

Miners headlamps in the darkness of the cage.

The descent picked out by their lights. Dark, light, dark.

Out of the darkness we see sweating bodies wading through slime, their bare backs bent by the roof.

Jamie slams the main door shut. Again shutting out the light. He progresses across the kitchen towards an inner door. As he lifts up the latch Mrs Knox is heard to say, though not unpleasantly

MRS KNOX Come away from there, son.

Jamie turns.

Mrs Knox can be seen beyond the open living room door. As usual she is seated by the fire and as usual she has her face averted.

MRS KNOX You're not allowed in there.

A numb face. Jamie drops the latch.

Jamie's old home. He reaches the top of the open stairs and on to the landing. He tries the door but it won't open. He batters the door in anguish.

Jamie, a tiny figure crouched on the earth.

Closer, Jamie's intent face.

A beautiful white fernlike flower with butterfly. The creature flits into space.

Jamie rear view. He shoulders his braces. Then he heels back the earth the way an animal does when it covers its waste.

A winter's day. Slush high in gutters. Frozen villagers queuing along the pavement and up an open stair, kettles and pails and jugs in their hands. A woman called Agnes descends the stairs with two vessels of water in a yoke.

Jamie is standing outside the door. The blind is drawn behind him.

Agnes is now inside her doorway. She eyes Jamie for a moment then foots her door to a close.

Hunting for mother's pearls

The two neighbouring houses. Jamie hurries away, progressing behind the building.

A rear window. There are hints of wartime sticky tape still on the window pane. Agnes is there, watching from behind the glass, or rather trying to watch now

As Jamie's leg slips inside his own window.

The empty living room in the firelight. In the distance, in a flood of icy daylight, framed in an open doorway, we can see Jamie disappear into the kitchen.

Inside the kitchen. An arrangement of bottles on a shelf with all their liquid levels marked.

Jamie drinking from a bottle of milk.

He goes to the water tap, turns the handle, but no luck. The tap is dry. A worried Jamie.

Mrs Knox doddering through an alleyway with the whippet on a lead.

Jamie peeing into the whippet's sleeping basket beside the fire.

The milk bottle safely back on the shelf at its correct level.

The soaking dog's basket. Sudden sound of the key turning in the lock.

Jamie alarmed.

The boy scurries back in the direction he came. But no, the door is opening, too late. He slips under the table by the window.

Mrs Knox ambles into the room. She is drunk. She turns an eagle eye and sees

Beyond the bedroom door the window is open. Jamie doesn't know it yet but she has eyes in the back of her head.

She goes to poke the fire and a blaze of light fills the room. She turns, looks down, exclaims

MRS KNOX What have you done?

Jamie's cautious face in shadow under the table. Hears

MRS KNOX My poor darling.

Sees

Mrs Knox sitting in her chair kissing the whippet on the mouth.

The door is lying open.

Jamie draws on his bootlace. When he looks again at his grandmother he gets a shock.

Her hand is outstretched towards him while the rest of her remains invisible. She twiddles her fingers to emphasise her invitation.

Jamie comes out from under the table and moves timidly towards her. Her face is lit up by the fire. She listens to his progress instead of turning. She takes Jamie's hand and draws him in front of her. Then she brings the boy to her breast and smothers him in a warm embrace. She speaks with much affection.

MRS KNOX Who is the best boy in all the wide world?

Jamie's face squeezed against her breast.

MRS KNOX Who is it, my darling?

Jamie opens an eye on

The abandoned whippet. The creature looks rejected.

Mrs Knox's cheeks are wet. She caresses her head against Jamie's hair with a display of great emotion.

MRS KNOX My young prince.

Moonlight beyond the closed window, and moonlight touching where Jamie lies on the pillow. He says very quietly

JAMIE Please Jesus make granny drunk every night.

Then he closes his eyes. He looks peaceful.

Morning light. The antler horns in shadow on the wall.

Jamie is standing in his usual corner by the living room door and looking as confused as ever.

Mrs Knox is as usual by the fire. She says quite calmly

MRS KNOX I got word from the asylum.

She lets the whippet lick her face.

MRS KNOX Your mother's dead.

Jamie, a numb face.

Mrs Knox is now in profile. She says with genuine consideration

MRS KNOX Whatever misfortunes she had in her life she didn't deserve that.

Jamie goes under the table.

Mrs Knox has her face turned away. Her hand is extended towards the boy but this time it holds a letter, the envelope of which is unopened.

Classroom. A boy, Archie, is standing before the class reading from his composition. All others have their backs to us, including the teacher who sits in Archie's place.

ARCHIE There is more beauty than horror in our countryside, more hope than despair. If you get stung by a bee you can cure it with the docken leaf because it has healing properties.

Archie closer.

ARCHIE There is a legend that says it is safe to take home anything from nature except one thing. This is called Dead Men's Flourish . . .

Very close, Jamie, daydreaming, hearing

ARCHIE If you take home this flower it means somebody will die.

A profusion of this white fernlike dead men's flourish shivering in the wind.

Mrs Knox fast asleep in bed.

Jamie's hand slipping a sprig of this flower beneath her bed, its petals given an eerie hue by the moonlight.

Jamie closing the door silently behind him.

A white ambulance travelling down a sunny country road.

Jamie's intent face round a street corner.

The ambulance is stationed outside the front door. Sudden signs of life in movement. The window of the house slides open. The vehicle doors swing open. A stretcher bearing someone is being carried from the vehicle.

Jamie stunned.

The stretcher entering the house by the open window.

Jamie moving swiftly on tip-toe towards the rear window. He peers carefully inside.

Through the window, inside the empty silent room there is an old man lying in bed. There is a strange remoteness in his frail body. This is Old Mr Knox, who is Mrs Knox's husband.

The firelit living room is silent too. Mrs Knox's fireside chair is empty. She is discovered lying on top of her bed with a newspaper covering her face.

Jamie peering inside the living room door. Nearby, in the middle of the table there is a plate with two apples. Jamie turns to look at the fruit.

The whippet looks up from beside its sleeping mistress and follows Jamie's progression.

Jamie closing the bedroom door quietly behind him.

The dog sits bolt upright as if it knew Jamie was doing wrong.

Jamie is standing beside his grandfather's bed, watching.

The old man's eyes have a look of deep impenetrable hurt in them.

Jamie seems to understand. He puts the apple on the bed.

Suddenly there comes a sound of angry movement.

Jamie turns alarmed.

Behind the closed door, more sounds of Mrs Knox but coming nearer.

Old Mr Knox's hopeless face.

Jamie dropping into the street, closing the window, hurrying away.

Old Mr Knox is accompanied by Agnes. They are in a field by a dried up stream. Agnes has her hand in a comforting way on top of the old man's and they are quite content just to be peaceful, both lost in their own thoughts.

AGNES The electric treatment did you good.

The old man nods.

Agnes pats his hand.

AGNES I'd have dropped in to see you but you know what she's like.

The old man sighs.

Agnes looks away across the grass then back slightly amused. She says in a secret way

AGNES He's wondering who I am.

Jamie is watching from behind a tree trunk. Old Mr Knox turns affectionately to look at the boy. Agnes does likewise. She is still studying Jamie after the old man has turned back. Jamie, feeling the woman's solitary gaze, hides himself. Old Mr Knox has been looking at Agnes's breast which is amply revealed. Finally, Agnes turns back. She obviously thinks there is something peculiar about Jamie.

AGNES He's alright, is he?

The old man decides to change the subject. With a saucy smile he whispers into Agnes's ear. She laughs and adjusts her apron.

AGNES You haven't changed a bit.

Jamie sneaks another look.

Agnes is going. The pit horn is blowing in the distance and it hurries her down a slope and out of view.

John sneaks a look round the living room door.

Mrs Knox is snoozing in her chair.

Agnes is standing outside her house as if she was waiting for something. She turns surreptitiously, sees

John behind the kitchen window. He makes a secret sign language to her. Points to himself, then to her, then to an imaginary watch, then holds up five fingers.

Agnes gets the message. She indicates with eyes that Jamie is around.

We see Jamie crouched on the ground idly playing with some pebbles, and John in the background. John disappears from view.

Agnes closes her door.

Jamie hasn't been looking until now, until the sound of the door clacking. He looks there, then the other way where John was, and we know he hasn't missed a thing. He goes back to his game and draws two pebbles together.

Jamie and his grandfather warmed by the sun in the field by the dried up stream. The old man rubs an apple on his jacket, then hands it to Jamie. Jamie is content to eat the fruit while his grandfather stares into space lost in a private world of his own. Then the old man speaks out of a memory of something fond.

OLD MR KNOX Your mother. She was a very nice girl. Always remember that, son.

He drifts back inside himself for a moment thinking about her and his face warms.

OLD MR KNOX She was so full of life. When she smiled, when she smiled the sun was born in her eyes. I thought the world of her.

Then his face saddens thinking of what became of her.

JAMIE Grandad?

The old man puts his arm round the boy.

JAMIE Grandad, your wife isn't very good to you. Is she?

The old man laughs at the boy's insight.

The sun in the sky is radiant. Then it disappears behind a dark cloud.

Jamie is sitting on the stair landing. He is reading his letter. A mucky crumpled envelope lies in his lap. Tommy reads the letter for him.

> Dear Jamie just a few lines to let you know how I am keeping. Well I am keeping well. My da' came to see me then he never came back. If he comes again I am going to ask him to bring you . . .

Mr Brown, Tommy's father, exits from the village school followed by Jamie. The children are heard inside the school.

> A man came to talk to me about a career in the army. But I don't care about anything . . .

Mr Brown's Austin journeying along a country road.

> The home is not bad so long as you learn to look out for yourself. . .

The Austin lost in a busy street in the city.

> From what I can see it's every man for himself. . .

Rushing passers-by.

> They would take your head if it wasn't fixed on your shoulders. . .

The stationary car and towering above it a dark Victorian building.

> I'm wearing long trousers now. That is all I have to say.

Tommy emerges through swing doors in his longs. He is neither a boy nor a man, but he has the mannerisms of the adult even if somewhat awkward. The swing doors are left rattling to and fro.

Mr Brown looks awkward as if forced to come more out of duty than a desperate need to see his son. But he says

MR BROWN Hello, son.

Mr Brown is sitting on a bed in a corridor of beds. Jamie is sitting on another with his back to us. Tommy is standing in a couldn't-care-less attitude. He doesn't reply to his father but he goes and, careful to pull up his trouser knees, sits beside the man. There is a momentary silence while Mr Brown thinks of something to say.

MR BROWN Well, how are you doing, son?

Tommy shrugs, winks across at Jamie.

Jamie gives a brief smile.

MR BROWN I had a word with the wife. . .

Previous page: Burying the pearls in coal dust

While Mr Brown stutters his way through his words, Tommy picks his pocket.

MR BROWN It isn't that we ... Well, you know how it is. You're getting on to being a man now.

Tommy offers his father one of his own Woodbines, then he has one himself. Mr Brown lights them up. He is due to lose the matches beside other things.

MR BROWN It's just that ... Well, you'd be strange to the kids. And them being set in their ways. You know. But I'll come and see you.

Tommy twiddles the box of matches secretly.

Jamie amused.

Mr Brown offers his son a pound note which has been in his hand all the time.

Tommy shakes his head.

Mr Brown looks awkward. He didn't expect that response. He wavers the note around, not knowing quite what to do with it. Finally he puts it in the same pocket Tommy has been tapping.

Behind a frosted window, Mr Brown is in earnest conversation with an official.

Tommy and Jamie are sitting on the bed facing each other.

Jamie is drawing badly on a cigarette. Tommy leans forward to whisper in his ear.

Tommy laughs at his own joke. He blows air into a contraceptive. We can see his father in the distance. Jamie points the tip of his cigarette on the balloon and it bursts.

Jamie laughs.

Mr Knox disappearing round a corner of the village. He is on a bicycle.

Jamie watching.

Mr Knox re-emerges some distance away. There is no sound except for a loose mudguard clanking away. Then the man finally disappears for good. It is rather like a game of 'first you see me, now you don't'. But the sound lingers.

Mrs Knox sitting in her usual chair by the fire. She turns to profile and says kindly

MRS KNOX Help yourself to an apple.

Jamie in his usual corner and not too sure of his ground.

A solitary apple on a plate and beside it a mousetrap set for action.

JAMIE I don't like apples.

Mrs Knox again has her hand outstretched towards him.

Old Mr Knox listening behind the bedroom door. He looks worried.

Jamie and his grandmother facing each other. She has the boy gently by the hand. She puts a finger to her mouth and whispers

MRS KNOX Sssh. There's a mouse listening.

She listens herself, then smiles to Jamie, at the same time drawing him into her confidence.

MRS KNOX Do you know what pearls look like?

Jamie thinks, nods.

MRS KNOX Do you know where your mother kept them?

Jamie thinks again, nods.

MRS KNOX Bring them to me and I'll look after them.

She slips a key inside Jamie's fingers.

The open stairs leading up to the landing.

Jamie is kneeling inside the bedcupboard.

Granny bribing Jamie with an apple

There is a striped pillow ballooned between his knees. He plunges a knife into the material.

A portrait of Jamie's mother on the wall. A gentle sad face.

A storm of feathers snowing about the room

And on to the bare wooden floor. And of course the string of pearls.

Jamie burying the pearls in coal dust on the slag heap. Then he hurries away.

A world of black ash. And the pearls hidden forever.

At the picture house. Today: *I Didn't Do It*. A beaming George Formby.

Jamie, clonking jam jars in hand, enters the cinema foyer.

A blazing fire

That flares on the walls of the room. Mrs Knox invisible as usual. John and Jamie face to face.

John draws his face closer to Jamie. His voice is calm. He has a friendly hand on the boy's shoulder.

JOHN You're lying.

A shrinking Jamie.

JAMIE I couldn't find them.

John almost fatherly.

JOHN You know what happens to laddies who tell lies? They go to hell.

Suddenly, John pulls Jamie up by the hair.

Mrs Knox unmoved by the sounds of a terrifying agony, by the pulling and pushing and punching within her reach. Jamie screams as if he was about to die.

Then in a sizzling flash his head touches the fire grating. His body held there by this hero's hands. And now there is no sound and the boy's mouth and eyes are bulging as if petrified forever.

The whippet curled up in a soft lap.

John closes the door silently behind him.

Mrs Knox draws the hurt boy to her breast. Jamie lets his face smother in her warmth, lets himself be cradled. He gives out a high-pitched whine like a wounded dog. When Mrs Knox speaks she means every word she says.

MRS KNOX Granny loves you, darling, granny loves you, granny loves you.

Jamie understands nothing.

That night. Moonlight lies on the pillow with John. He puffs on a cigarette and its smoke hovers in the still room. Jamie lies in shadow next to him, face away to the wall. Old Mr Knox's bed is empty beyond.

John says quite calmly

JOHN Breathe a word and I'll kill you.

Jamie's hurt face staring at the wall.

Early morning light in the room. Old Mr Knox comes wearily through the bedroom door, back from the pit, his face coal-black. The jagged antler horns are there, in shadow, charging down from the wall above him.

Jamie is lying awkwardly sprawled across his grandfather's bed. The covers hang off him in a twisted heap. A mucky smudge of dried tears lies on his still face.

The old man stands there looking at the boy. Then, because he really cares, he very gently draws up the covers.

White flames in a cold grey street.

At the foot of the open staircase there is a huge blazing fire. The place is deserted. Then sudden movement

As a sweating John comes on to the stair landing. He struggles with the rocking chair which he throws over the railings.

Smouldering ashes and silence.

Jamie, a demented-looking creature at his school desk, head on arm, eyes that stare into space in the manner of his grandfather.

The whole class, rear view. A very animated teacher is talking about the earth in relation to other planets, but the sound is coming as if from a million light years away. On the blackboard are drawn the planets in space.

The planets isolated.

We journey into real space and see an insignificant world. This circle, this terribly shining beautiful and silent thing that can hold so much pain.

A door crashes shut. We are at the corner by the living room door where Jamie usually waits. Mrs Knox is there. She has a friendly hand on Jamie's and the other on the door which she shut.

Old Mr Knox is seated at the table with food before him. But he is no longer eating. He is rock-still. It is as if the crashing door had caught him. His spoon is suspended above his plate and his eyes have a desperate look in them.

Mrs Knox is now sitting with her back to us as usual. She still holds on to Jamie's hand where he stands next to her. But the boy is turned to his grandfather's direction. Mrs Knox doesn't move when she speaks. Her tone is the kind that comes from a smile on a bitter face.

MRS KNOX Off to see your old flame, are you? Mmm?

No answer.

Jamie looks more and more nervous.

MRS KNOX Off to get her sympathy. Mmm?

Still no answer.

MRS KNOX Can't wait to get on top of her?

Mrs Knox turns her face to profile.

MRS KNOX Mmm?

The old man hasn't moved. Then he says something in a way that suggests he has said it all many times before.

OLD MR KNOX It's all in your imagination.

Mrs Knox, front view but still in profile, Jamie, and in the background, on his side, his grandfather. The woman smiles knowingly to herself.

A bee buzzing frantically against the window pane.

Mrs Knox has Jamie's face held tenderly in the palms of her hands and they are very close together. You sense her own desperate loneliness, her need for someone to listen.

MRS KNOX He thought I didn't know about his whore all these long years.

She shakes her head pathetically. Then with a sense of victory

MRS KNOX But I never let him touch me. No, not once. Not once.

She covers her face with her hands, becomes involved with herself. She shakes her head, nursing herself. Jamie backs away. Mrs Knox begins to cry. When she speaks it comes in an agonised high-pitched whimper.

MRS KNOX He never cared for me.

Jamie closes the door silently behind him.

Mrs Knox cries bitterly into her hands. The whippet paddies on to her lap.

The old man still hasn't moved. There is nothing to say any more.

Archie, the schoolboy, comes out of Agnes's house pushing a bike. He stops to look with more than passing interest at something, then says

ARCHIE You're wearing my shirt.

Jamie is crouched head in arms outside his own door. He doesn't look up.

Neighbouring houses as Archie rides away. When he has gone, there is still the sound of the bike's loose mudguard clanking

In Jamie's ear. Now the boy looks up above his arms.

The house Archie has just left. The blind is drawn.

The rear windows of the house. Jamie is hovering about outside the one with the hint of wartime sticky tape on its panes. He sneaks a look inside.

Beyond him, in the silent room lie Agnes and John in bed.

At that moment, Archie and an irate Mr Knox and bike emerge from an alley.

Close, Jamie watching his father and Archie, his step-brother.

Jamie, rear view, foreground, watching the figures in the distance. Then he turns his back on them, sees

His grandfather up on the railway embankment. The boy makes after him calling

Jealous fury: Granny attacking Agnes

JAMIE Grandad!

He scurries up the grassy slope.

JAMIE Grandad!

But the old man doesn't seem to hear.

Jamie and his grandfather are sitting where they usually sit, in the field by the dried-up stream. The old man looks wretched. The boy has his head in the old man's lap.

OLD MR KNOX Don't you think you would be happier in a home?

Jamie says nothing.

His grandfather then says with a terrible feeling of helplessness

OLD MR KNOX Grandad hasn't the strength to fight for you, son.

The dried-up stream.

The flames flit over the walls of the living room as if it was on fire. Mr Knox has his face buried in his mother's lap. He is crying bitterly. Mrs Knox pulls her son up by the hair.

Her face looks demoniacal.

MRS KNOX Forget the whore, forget her! She doesn't exist!

Mr Knox's pathetic tear-stained face, hearing

MRS KNOX You're a King. The whole world is yours. You must never give up. Never!

Then with extreme tenderness

MRS KNOX I believe in you, my darling, I believe in you. The whole world is yours. Go and find a woman worthy of you.

She kisses her son on the mouth with passion.

Jamie watching under the table.

Jamie hurries through the rain towards the door. At that moment Mrs Knox opens the door. She thrusts an apple in Jamie's hand and shushes him away. Then having closed the door, she turns the key in the lock.

We see Mr Knox sitting at the table, which is now set and in the centre of the room.

We see Old Mr Knox entering this room. He closes the bedroom door behind him. He is completely absorbed in himself. He is dressed for going out.

The whole room as Old Mr Knox makes his exit. There are three figures at the table, Mr Knox, his mother and

Helen, who is Mr Knox's new find. Helen is a refined, clean-looking, attractive girl. She looks like an outsider. She has the shyness that visitors of her kind usually have. And there is a kind of innocence about her. Helen is the only person who isn't animated.

She looks somewhat uncomfortable in the silence left behind after Old Mr Knox's departure.

Mr Knox looks to his mother. And for the benefit of Helen, Mrs Knox puts her index finger to her temple to suggest that all is not well with the old man.

Helen gives an embarrassed smile. Mr Knox places a comforting hand on Helen's shoulder.

Suddenly Mrs Knox isn't looking at all happy.

There is a string of pearls hanging round Helen's neck.

The antler's jagged horns.

Old Mr Knox is standing with his back to us. He is stillness itself. There is no warm light from the sun. And there is no sound except for the rhythmic chug and sway of an approaching train.

The old man is standing in the middle of the railway tracks. Suddenly the train thunders through a tunnel in clouds of steam.

But the engine runs on another track, by-passing the harrowed figure. Then the last wagon goes, leaving in its wake a gust of cold wind.

Mrs Knox crashes the door shut on the darkness outside. There is a momentary pause, then the same door flies open. Mrs Knox throws some underclothing away from her, shouting

MRS KNOX Don't come back!

Final door crash.

John is standing in the crazy moonlight surrounded by his belongings, soldier's uniform and all. Agnes is standing at her open doorway engulfed in a blaze of light.

The crazy moon.

Agnes throws a bundle of clothes into the air and laughs like a schoolgirl at the circus of her day. She falls against John and laughs helplessly.

Mrs Knox, a still figure at the open door.

Suddenly, Mrs Knox goes for Agnes like a panther for its prey. We are looking into the arena of raw emotion now. They tear at one another, abuse one another, while John does a disappearing act into Agnes's house, and young Archie comes from it to his mother's defence. The boy is not heard above the madness.

Jamie watching from behind the window.

In the morning. Silence. Mrs Knox is in an embrace with her son. He moves away with his mother's hand trailing along his arm. She holds on to his wrist. He breaks away. She moves her hand to the base of her neck.

Mr Knox progresses towards the front of an open lorry, in the rear of which there are odds and ends of furniture. Prominent amongst this is the table beneath which Jamie used to hide.

Mr Knox climbs into the cabin where his girlfriend Helen is waiting, and slams the door shut.

Agnes's house showing no signs of life. Sounds of the lorry driving away.

Mrs Knox waves until there is silence, then her arm falls by her side. She looks worried. Her fingers are smoothing an imaginary string of pearls round her neck.

The jagged points of the antler's horns relieved by moonlight. Silence.

Jamie awkwardly asleep.

A padded door. Sounds of hissing gas.

Old Mr Knox curled up on the kitchen floor like a foetus.

In the soundless room, Mrs Knox lies peacefully asleep with her dog beside her. The bedroom door lies open and beyond that an open window.

The coffin coming into the daylight street through an open window.

Jamie, a still figure grieving by the dried-up stream.

The hearse moving slowly and silently uphill.

Happy laughing children at play.

Jamie far away, separate. He appears to have turned in the process of walking away. Their carefree sound is dying in him.

Ecstatic sight and sound of these children, gloriously at one with their childhood.

Jamie very far away, still watching, but after further progression. Their sound is dead in him. Then he turns and he goes away through an alley and there is silence.

The window blind is drawn. The door lies open. There is a stationary black van outside the house. Jamie comes willingly out of the house accompanied by a charity worker who closes the door behind him. Then another uniformed worker comes into view. Jamie lets the man lift him into the vehicle. The man follows and his companion closes the doors.

The van travelling along the country road towards the city.

A steep street close to the city. There is a swirling pipe band coming on the descent. They are playing 'Scotland Forever'. They are trailed by patriots singing with great fervour

> Let the Irish sing of the Emerald Isle
> Where the three leaf shamrock grows
> Let the English praise their valleys
> And their dales
> And the bonnie blooming rose...

The van appears on the other side of the road but going in an opposite direction, upwards.

And they sing

> But give me the land of the heather and the kilt
> The mountains and the rivers
> For the blood leaps in my veins
> When I hear the bagpipes playing
> Scotland
> Dear old Scotland
> Forever...

And on they go on their triumphant way.

> Scotland
> Dear old Scotland
> Forever.

The van turns a corner at the top of the hill, still travelling upwards.

And the music dies away on the empty street.

Previous page: The hearse taking Grandfather away

Portrait of the royal family. The Queen has a child on her lap.

Framed nativity, mother and child. An angel comes to place a star above them. The three wise men appear. They speak out with boyish enthusiasm.

FIRST WISE MAN It has been a long tiring journey.

SECOND WISE MAN Many evil things have been sent to try us.

THIRD WISE MAN But we didn't give up.

The Provost has given up. He is asleep. A gloved hand comes to nudge him and he opens his eyes.

Out in the corridor, Jamie stands bored. He is dressed in a kilt and is holding a bouquet.

The sound of applause comes up.

Hands on his hips, Mr Bridge confronts the boy. He sighs. He puts out his hand as much as to say, get on with it.

The door opens. Jamie comes in.

The Provost, his wife and daughter, stand waiting.

Jamie comes forward. And as he does so the legs of his trousers slowly slide down below his kilt.

MY WAY HOME

There are cheers as the children jump up

And silence as the balloons float down.

Jamie, a pathetic head on a pillow. There is no other sound except his own small disturbed breathing. His hands are curled up in front of his cheeks like a child in embryo.

The dormitory dwarfs him. Out on the stairs, through frosted glass, a light clicks on. There are Christmas decorations.

In the distance we can hear church bells.

Mr Bridge enters through the swing doors.

He is carrying a bag of goodies.

One boy has left a letter addressed to Dear Santa. In reply Mr Bridge deposits a small package in Christmas wrapping.

A sock hangs at the foot of a bed and he drops another small package into it.

Trousers hang at the foot of another bed and when the small package drops, we see that the legs are tied with string.

Silently, hands unwrap a package and the object shines in the darkness.

It is morning. On the stairs Jamie is intently hammering a nail with his shoe.

Closer, we see he has been marking his name on a brand-new shiny mouth-organ.

He raises it to his lips and blows.

In the empty hallway there is a cacophony.

In the dining hall, it seems that every boy has a mouth-organ.

MR BRIDGE Quiet!

He looks stern. But from the breast pocket of his jacket, he takes out a mouth-organ of his own and gives it a quick blow up and down the scale. He looks pleased with himself.

MR BRIDGE We will now say grace. For what we are about to receive . . .

On the table, there are plates of Christmas pudding and cups of tea.

MR BRIDGE May the Lord make us truly thankful. For Jesus Christ's sake . . .

His hands are clenched in prayer.

MR BRIDGE Amen.

Jamie is eating at the dining table, surrounded by a clatter of utensils.

The table is full of boys, all identically dressed. They are engrossed in the business of feeding healthy appetites.

A member of staff at the children's home, Mr Bridge is everything his job expects of him. He can be as strict as a teacher or as lenient as a father but is always dressed immaculately to match the former. At the moment he is dealing with a boy – we will call him Andrew – who is not eating and who looks very sorry for himself.

MR BRIDGE What's the matter, son, eh? You won't grow into a big chap if you don't eat.

He is patiently coaxing the boy to eat. The boy holds back, obviously playing up for the man's affection.

MR BRIDGE Andrew, what's the matter, son? Come and sit over at my table, eh? It will be nicer.

Jamie is now no longer eating. His spoonful is suspended above his plate as if he had changed his mind. He is perfectly still, watching, listening.

MR BRIDGE Let's try a spot of this stuff.

The boys on either side of Jamie take no notice. And neither it seems does Mr Bridge. To make matters worse he is becoming too close and too attentive to the ailing Andrew.

MR BRIDGE Good boy. Good lad. I thought you'd lost the use of your arms just now.

Jamie has given up the idea of eating altogether. The plate has been discarded. He is in a huff with his sulking head leaning on his sulking hand.

MR BRIDGE Good boy. Splendid. I'll play you a tune while you're eating, eh? Music while you eat.

Jamie swipes his eating things off the table.

Sound of plates crashing.

A flash of Jamie crashing out of the door,

Up the stairs

And through the swing doors.

The whole dining hall, silent, static, alerted. There is a tremendous clatter above their heads.

Jamie is lying on his bed in his usual manner curled up like a foetus.

Inside the dormitory the door is barricaded.

Sound of concerned footsteps coming up the stairs. Whoever comes in is going to have to wrench two beds aside. But Mr Bridge has absolutely no trouble at all opening the door since it also swings outwards.

Later Jamie comes out of the swing doors, down the stairs

And into the empty dining hall. He crouches on the floor to pick up the broken pieces.

Mr Bridge is sitting at his office desk. He has been studying a report.

MR BRIDGE Oh, he's doing very well. Very well.

There is no movement except for his fingers tapping out an irritable rhythm on the wood. He looks up and says

MR BRIDGE Your interest is a bit late, don't you think?
Jamie's father is sitting across the other side of the desk. He knows he is on the right side. But he answers reasonably

FATHER Ah well, he's still my son, isn't he?

His collar is too tight. He slips his index finger inside and pulls. Then using the free hand he wavers it through the air and says

FATHER When all's said and done.

The hand is now quite still, its palm wide open in a gesture of helplessness. And we get the feeling that whatever this man has done or not done in the past, things will be different.

MR BRIDGE So you want to make amends?

Judging by the look on his face he has seen it all before.

MR BRIDGE Your son wants to be a painter.

FATHER Aye, well, there's always plenty houses need painting.

MR BRIDGE He wants to paint pictures.

FATHER Is that what he's good at?

MR BRIDGE He should go to an art school.

The father takes a bag of sweets out of his pocket and inserts one into his mouth.

'You look like a gentleman': Jamie's first job

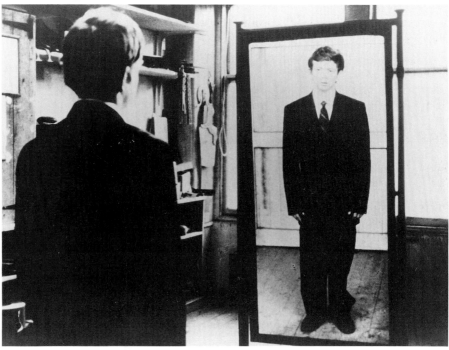

FATHER That's alright with me. Education is a great thing.

Jamie is sitting outside the office. Apart from biting at his finger-nail he is quite still. His father is seen behind the frosted glass like a character in a shadow play. He gestures with his hand but nothing is heard. He disappears out of view.

Into view, behind clear glass, comes Helen. She is outside the building. She peers inside like the stranger she is. But more of her later.

The office door opens and out comes the boy's father. Jamie gets up. Man and boy face each other for a moment. The father gives the bag of sweets to his son. Then he ruffles the boy's hair affectionately and, with a brushing gesture, directs him towards the office. Jamie leaves the door open behind him. Mr Bridge promptly closes it. The man is left sitting in the chair vacated by his son. He looks a bit uncomfortable, as if he had put on his Sunday-best and his best behaviour for the occasion. He does his best to ignore a tapping sound at the window.

Helen is watching from behind the clear glass. She is the visitor's girlfriend. She looks strained and her unkempt appearance suggests she is no longer interested in herself or life for that matter. But there is something at odds with her drab appearance for she supports a string of pearls. She chews at a bead the way others chew a finger-nail. She taps the glass. No reaction. She taps again, irritably, and, getting a reaction, indicates impatience, rat-a-tat-tats her finger at her wrist, though there is no watch there.

Jamie's father is on his feet. He looks quickly about him to see no one is looking, then springs into a sudden fury of life. His legs do a crazy dance while his arms thrust the air. His mouth looks as if it was shouting but nothing is heard. Suddenly he becomes rock-still and now there is only one hand thrusting and it moves the way it would if he was opening a curtain in anger. Then he is back in the chair with his hands dramatically holding on to his head.

Helen runs down the street out of view.

Jamie and Mr Bridge are sitting together. The desk is there but it doesn't supply a barrier between them.

MR BRIDGE We might as well face it, he has never in all his life done anything for you, has he, son? He left the job of looking after you to his old mother. And she didn't exactly put out the welcome home flag.

Jamie doesn't look at Mr Bridge, who is full of concern.

MR BRIDGE Look, I'll be quite frank with you, Jamie. I'm not too happy about your going back.

He thinks for a moment, becomes quite lively.

MR BRIDGE Anyway, for all our ups and downs, I imagine you would miss me, wouldn't you, son?

He encloses his hand on Jamie's in a warming gesture. Jamie nods. The man taps the boy's hand and withdraws.

MR BRIDGE Look, I can't stop your father taking you.

He pauses for a moment.

MR BRIDGE On the other hand, you don't have to go, son.

Jamie slips a sweet in his mouth, carefully pockets the bag.

Mr Bridge sighs to himself. It's the old case of blood being thicker than water and no persuading in the world will change that.

The lorry journeying away down a slope in the city.

Jamie and his father do not speak. As they drive along, a barrel organ is heard playing 'Oh I Do Like to Be Beside the Seaside'.

The street ahead is deserted. We can see Helen waiting on the pavement. We can see her through the cabin window. She proceeds to the kerb, waits. Suddenly the vehicle gathers speed causing her to vanish. Then it brakes on the empty road ahead.

The lorry is now stationed some distance from Helen, who is having to run to catch up. To make matters worse, she is having to contend with the horn blasting.

Silence, except for the low purring sound of the engine. Jamie's father is at the driving wheel, completely absorbed in his own thoughts.

Jamie is all the time looking up at his father. Now he turns away and looks with equal concentration at the woman on the other side of him.

Her legs are clad in nylon stockings.

Helen is turned away in the opposite direction. Her head is leaning against the glass and her troubled gaze has a look of sad emptiness about it.

Jamie's gaze returns to his father. He is trying to put two and two together. Then he turns and looks straight ahead.

Countryside. A road. The lorry stops.

Helen emerges from the front of the lorry.

She walks away across the field.

The pearls lying abandoned on the seat. A hand gathers them up.

Jamie's father is standing on a bank. He moves his arm in a single curving gesture like a planter of seeds and frees himself of the pearls. They glide away from him

And lose themselves in water that is dank and dark and quite dead.

Agnes, a harried face. Agnes is Jamie's father's wife. She is out in the open air, has her arms folded, is looking down the village street.

The road into the village. We can hear the sound of the lorry and see it taking the corner.

The stationary lorry. Jamie's father steps on to the street, slams the cabin door shut.

Agnes turns her back, stampedes into the house and slams the door shut. We can see the window blind is drawn. And that the only movement is from a child's dress hanging on the line. Jamie and his father approach. On reaching the door, the man whispers something to Jamie. Then he goes in and closes the door, leaving the boy outside.

We remain with the waiting Jamie. We hear very heated words emanating from inside the house. It seems as if all hell is let loose. Suddenly, Archie throws open the door. He is upset, he shouts back inside

ARCHIE Da, what did you have to come back for?

Then he runs away. Archie is followed immediately by Agnes, who tears out as if she were on a battlefield. She is clutching a child in her arms. She screams

AGNES Archie!

The alarmed Jamie watches her go, watches her come back hugging tightly her broken-hearted son. They don't seem to notice Jamie because she slams the door like an earthquake. Then there is absolute silence.

The boy remains looking at this door wondering if his father will ever come. Out of the silence comes the small sound of a stick on glass. Jamie doesn't react. The sound, a sharper one, comes again.

Jamie turns a pathetic head to see

His grandmother, who is there behind her kitchen window. Her face has the kind of emaciated look that comes from premature ageing, from unendurable pain and loneliness. She moves away.

She opens the door to a slit suggesting invitation but there is no sign of her.

Her house neighbours that of Agnes. Jamie is looking towards this house with its open door and its window that has a look of desolation about it. He enters the house, cautiously accepting the invitation.

His grandmother is sitting beside her empty hearth. Her hands are wrapped up in mountains of soiled black ointment-smeared bandages, giving her frail body a deformed look. She looks dirty from lack of attention. But a clean new book, a large one, the kind children read, lies open in her lap.

There is a pen poised awkwardly in her hand and she is lost deep in thought. She proceeds to write something on a blank white page.

The room is sparse and cold and uncared for. The carpet or curtains or any other item that might offer comfort have been rolled up or put away.

Jamie is in a state of suspense waiting in a corner of the room. He is neither in the room nor out of the room. The door is open and he hovers there with his finger still depressed on the latch.

His grandmother has written, 'For my young prince, from his loving Grannie.'

She moves towards the boy with great difficulty. And as she goes we can see her feet are padded like her hands. Jamie puts out his hand to help her. But she shakes her head like a martyr. Finally, she meets up with the boy, hands him the book.

GRANDMOTHER Welcome home, son.

Jamie looks sadly at the gift book. He utters a small word in exchange.

Down and out at the Salvation Army hostel

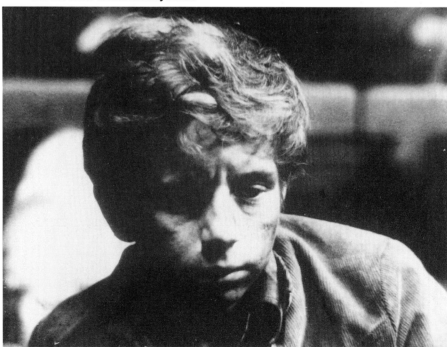

JAMIE Thanks.

It is a children's book called *David Copperfield*.

Jamie comes into his grandmother's house carrying a jug and a kettle. The room is no longer looking so sparse and cold and uncared for. All the haphazardness has gone. The room is back into shape, and there is a homely look about it.

Jamie puts the jug on the table and the kettle on the hob. He cleans up the grate and warms his hands for a moment. Then he goes to a drawer to polish the cutlery.

He polishes a knife until he can see his face in it.

He stands there, arms folded, in his grandmother's apron, surveying his work, humming happily to himself 'Oh I do Like to be Beside the Seaside'.

On the fireside chair lies his copy of *David Copperfield*.

Jamie comes out of the house carrying his book. He carefully closes the door and walks off. A moment later, Agnes comes out of the neighbouring house.

AGNES Jamie!

Jamie stops by the steps with his back to her.

AGNES Have you got something inside your belly?

Jamie does not look at her. But he nods his head and runs off.

He runs up the steps of an empty house. It is the house where he once lived with his maternal grandmother and Tommy. All the windows are broken. He sits in the sun to read his book.

As he turns the page there is an illustration of David Copperfield being beaten.

FATHER Jamie!

Jamie continues reading. His father shouts again.

FATHER Jamie!

Someone throws a stone at the boy engrossed in his book.

It is Archie. Now his father shouts at him.

FATHER Any more of that, my boy, and I'll boot your arse for you.

Archie throws another stone.

FATHER What did I tell you?

ARCHIE Go to hell!

He spits and walks off.

At the foot of the steps, Jamie's father has his arm around the boy's shoulder.

FATHER You shouldn't have run away like that. The wife was only trying to help. She's made up a bed for you.

Clutching his book, Jamie looks down at the ground.

FATHER Come on, son.

JAMIE I want to stay with my gran.

His father sighs.

Outside his grandmother's house the door is slightly ajar. We can hear a woman crying.

Jamie is standing inside the door. There is a moment's silence, then his grandmother speaks out of self-pity

GRANDMOTHER Why did you want to remove my name?

The room is dim. It is as if everything is uncared for again.

JAMIE I didn't. It just faded.

She breaks into self-pitying sobs. He hears her say again

GRANDMOTHER Why did you want to remove my name?

He smoothes his hand over the page of the book.

JAMIE It just faded.

She generates an unforeseen energy.

GRANDMOTHER You want the world to think I never cared for you.

Jamie looks more and more agonised.

JAMIE It's a nice present.

The boy feels as if his head will burst. He hears her accuse him again.

GRANDMOTHER Why did you want to hurt me?

He is staring down at the open gift book in his hand. He looks disturbed, hamstrung.

JAMIE I didn't do it.

There is a moment's silence. Everything is still. Suddenly Jamie gives way to a kind of madness.

In a flash his hand wrenches one page from the book, then another.

And now he is a demented thing in the room, ripping the gift book apart, screaming

JAMIE I didn't do it, I didn't do it, I didn't do it.

An explosion of coals on to a moving belt.

Jamie's father is in the gangway talking to the gaffer. His facial movements are very exaggerated in order to be heard above the din. He uses his index finger to point downwards towards the earth, then the thumb of the same hand over his shoulder indicating

Jamie, who is crouched in the coal outside the shed.

Jamie, a dark depressed face.

ARCHIE You're not right in the head.

Archie is standing alongside Jamie.

ARCHIE My ma says you got it from your mother.

Their father signals from the entrance to the pit.

FATHER Here, you two. Get a move on, eh.

He disappears into the black.

We see the giant chimney belching smoke and the pit wheel whirring round.

Jamie is standing in the corner of his father's living room, a moody figure. His face is coal-black from the pit.

JAMIE I wanted to be an artist.

AGNES And what kind of a job is that?

His father, Agnes and Archie stare at him.

AGNES I've bloody well asked you a question.

The father turns and goes out of the room.

He takes himself into the lavatory and shuts the door behind him.

Agnes and Archie stare at Jamie in incomprehension.

ARCHIE He must think he's better than us.

His mother rounds on him.

AGNES You shut your bloody mouth.

He follows his father out of the room. We hear the door slam behind him.

Jamie remains in the corner, head lowered.

AGNES An artist? Don't come here with your high-falootin' ideas. You go and do an honest day's work and get some dirt on your hands.

Her voice resounds in his ears.

AGNES If you were meant to be different you would have been born different.

He raises his head and looks at her.

AGNES This is your place in life.

Mr Bridge is playing the piano.

Jamie sits on a bench alone.

He is back at the children's home where Mr Bridge is trying to organise a dance.

A row of girls are seated at one side of the hall chattering among themselves.

MR BRIDGE Come on, boys.

But his efforts appear to be in vain

For the boys sit idly opposite.

He gets up from the stool as the keys of the pianola continue playing.

Some of the girls are dancing with one another.

MR BRIDGE Okay, girls, after them!

There are shrieks as they chase after partners.

One girl approaches Jamie. But he shakes his head and gets up to go.

As he leaves the hall, Mr Bridge comes after him.

MR BRIDGE Jamie!

Jamie is lying on top of his bed, curled up like a foetus. He seems to be in a very depressed state. He covers his face with his hand.

JAMIE If I run or walk it doesn't make any difference.

Mr Bridge is sitting there on the adjacent bed. He says nothing. Just sits there listening.

JAMIE It always comes to the same thing in the end.

He falls silent, remains perfectly still. Mr Bridge takes his hand.

A Gentlemen's Tailors in Princes Street. We can see the castle reflected in the plate-glass window.

The shop assistant trundles a full-length mirror along the corridor

And into the Despatch Room.

Jamie is being fitted out for his new job.

ASSISTANT I think you might take a wee look at yourself.

Jamie looks at himself in the mirror.

ASSISTANT They may be a wee bit big for you. Still it's a pity to waste them.

The suit is undeniably too big for Jamie.

ASSISTANT Yes, I think you look pretty smart. You look like a gentleman.

Jamie is not at all sure about this new image of himself.

He comes out of the tradesman's entrance and slips the parcel into the bicycle basket. He cycles off.

Next thing we know, the bicycle is parked outside a gentlemen's convenience. As he comes up the steps, it appears that Jamie has changed back into his regular clothes. He throws the black tie into the rubbish basket.

Inside the cubicle he has deposited the suit.

Fettes. Fettes is an enormous cathedral-like Private School standing in acres of green pasture.

Leaving his bicycle at the ornamental gates, Jamie traipses up the steep driveway to deliver the parcel. In the background, there are boys playing rugger.

Jamie is standing in the drive looking lost. He looks at the parcel, studies the label. Just then a voice is heard saying

SCHOOLBOY What do you want?

We see the schoolboy in question. He is kilted. His manner is exaggeratedly posh.

JAMIE I'm looking for somebody called Gaskni.

The schoolboy pulls a face of immense incredulity.

SCHOOLBOY I beg your pardon?

Jamie feels he has only to raise his voice.

JAMIE Gaskni.

We hear the schoolboy say

SCHOOLBOY Let me see that.

We see his hand take the parcel.

SCHOOLBOY Good Lord! That's not Gaskni. That's Gascoigne, you fool.

The whistle blows on the rugby field.

On the War Memorial, a dying soldier raises his hand to the blatant white sky.

From out of the sky, the face of an angel.

The kindly-faced woman stands by the swing door of the dormitory, where she is joined by Mr Bridge. She is a stranger. She is small, so he is stooped to offer an ear as she whispers to him. She glances briefly across the room at

Jamie sitting on his bed. He has the look of someone who knows he is being discussed. He looks over his shoulder.

In the background we can see the visitor watching him. She smiles.

Orchard Avenue. A homely-looking suburban house in a garden.

Jamie is standing in a corner of this snug little room just inside the door, looking and feeling like a visitor.

The amiable woman is sitting very comfortably beside her warm fire. She appears to be at peace with the world. Even in repose her face contains a smile. She sits there quite still, lost in her own thoughts.

A gramophone record plays 'I Know That My Redeemer Liveth'.

The woman moves up from her chair.

Her amiable hands remove a dish containing several ripe apples and

Extend it towards Jamie. He takes an apple. She leaves the plate on the table right next to the boy and moves away. We can hear the soft sound of her nestling back into her chair. Jamie stands there staring at the object in his hand.

He sneaks a look at

The woman who now appears to have dozed off, no doubt content that her kind gesture will put his world to rights, bring him out in time.

Jamie slips the gift inside his jerkin. Then, keeping his eye on the giver, he moves his hand and taking one apple after another, he draws them into his jerkin until the apple dish is empty. Very quietly he turns and goes out of the door.

The woman's sleeping hand is lying motionless in her lap, in an open gesture of acceptance.

Previous page: 'Mister, can you watch my place?'

An apple tree stands bare in an orchard.

A group of down-and-outs stand in line before

The Salvation Army woman who sits at the desk.

SALVATION ARMY WOMAN Now then, lad, what do you want?

JAMIE A bed.

SALVATION ARMY WOMAN Three shillings a night.

This seems to have Jamie stumped. She turns to a male assistant.

SALVATION ARMY WOMAN I think you'd better put this young lad with the others.

Framed in the dining room hatch is a plate of porridge.

Jamie is a small figure looking for a place. He finds it next to a very old tramp who has a face that seems to be all beard. Jamie sits quite still staring at his gruel while the old man very happily munches away, even managing to splosh his beard with the stuff. He is busily licking his spoon when Jamie taps him on the arm.

JAMIE Mister?

TRAMP What is it, son?

The old man gives Jamie his fullest attention.

JAMIE Can you watch my place? I forgot my spoon.

The old man digs his spoon deep into Jamie's porridge.

TRAMP You can have mine, son. I'm finished.

Then he turns away content to lick his beard.

Jamie considers his porridge for a moment, then gives the old man a long incredulous look.

We hear the hatch roll down to a thundering close.

The dormitory is immense. The beds are uniformly laid out and they stretch as far as the eye can see. There is no sight of the band or the singers but we can hear them sing

> Running over, running over
> My cup's full and running over
> For the Lord's made me
> As happy as can be
> My cup's full and running over.

The place is night still and silent. Everyone is undercover.

Except for Jamie. He is curled up in his usual manner. He seems to be saying to himself over and over again

JAMIE I want to die, I want to die, I want to die.

But he doesn't. He emerges from the Salvation Army building. The street is deserted. He strolls down the street as if he was going someplace. He stops, about turns, looks the other way, then back. He seems directionless.

The road into the village.

The empty village street.

The father's house. Jamie appears, strolls across the pavement towards the door and knocks. A man answers the door. They share a brief conversation but we can't really make out what they are saying.

There is the distant sound of trains shunting.

On closer inspection the man reveals himself as a stranger. Jamie makes to move and the man closes the door.

Jamie: imprisoned at home . . .

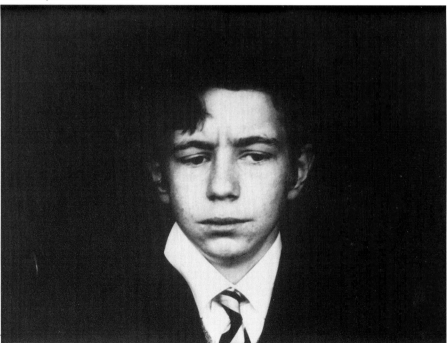

The boy progresses towards his grandmother's door, knocks. A woman answers. It is another stranger. Jamie moves away. The woman watches him go. Then she closes her door. Then there is silence.

The two houses. But it is all very different. All the windows have been bricked up and weeds grow everywhere.

Jamie, a desolate face on a station platform.

The departure hoarding is blank.

The railway lines criss-cross away into the night.

Sunlight. From the rear of a moving jeep, we see the tyre marks left in the desert sand. Then a village is passing and from it emanates the

Sound of native music.

We hear two disembodied voices.

JAMIE When was it you came out here then?

ROBERT What?

. . . liberated in Egypt

JAMIE When was it you came out here?

ROBERT When what? Oh, about a month before joining up with you lot.

JAMIE I'll show you around if you like.

ROBERT What?

JAMIE Don't you understand English?

ROBERT I beg your pardon?

JAMIE What's your name?

ROBERT Robert. What's yours?

JAMIE What?

ROBERT What is your name?

JAMIE Jamie.

Now we see Robert's face. And we are aware of other airmen lined up behind him on the parade ground. Robert, being the next in number, shouts

ROBERT FIFTEEN!

We remain on Robert's face as the continuing numbers now rapidly descend in volume. When eventually the number twenty-nine is heard we see

Jamie's face. And when he shouts the sound is immediate

JAMIE THIRTY!

We remain on Jamie's face while the sound of a sergeant's voice is yelling

SERGEANT Righ-ight TURN!

Jamie turns and the clacking sound of the others with him.

SERGEANT Le-eft TURN!

Pause.

SERGEANT A-bout TURN!

And again

SERGEANT A-bout TURN! By the left, Qui-ick MARCH!

Jamie moves forward and we hear the others with him and the sound of the band.

A limp Union Jack against the sky.

Once again we hear the sound of the Sergeant's voice

SERGEANT LE-EFT TURN!

Beyond the barbed wire there is a desert landscape. A silent place but for the band and the boots.

The Sergeant's voice is heard finally

SERGEANT LE-EFT WHEEL!

Jamie turns right. Oblivious to all, he wanders his own sweet way. And he is in a world of his own, for there is no sound to be heard now, nothing.

It is a quiet place where Jamie is kneeling on the sand. Before him there is a line of bricks, an open tin of white paint and a tin of black. He dips a paint brush and proceeds to paint one of the bricks black. He glances to one side

And we see that he has already painted a line of bricks that seems to stretch to infinity.

A stone.

Presently Robert approaches the stone. He looks small by comparison. He touches its surface, then backs away, leaving it.

An immense Pyramid made of the same stones.

Robert, an ecstatic face. He looks as if he were searching for a word to describe what he feels. He can't. He utters

ROBERT Well, what do you think of it?

He turns expectantly

To include Jamie. But Jamie is too busy fumbling around for matches to light up.

Robert is almost beside himself.

ROBERT Enthuse.

Jamie is standing there, cigarette in hand, like a thief caught in the act.

ROBERT ENTHUSE!!

But Jamie's face remains quite passive even when he hears Robert exclaim

ROBERT You're looking at one of the seven wonders of the WORLD!

A barbed-wire fence separates the camp from the desert.

To one side of the billet the sand is a mess except for a broad outer band. This band appears to encircle the building. Out of the silence comes a gentle sound of scraping. Then the appearance of Jamie. He comes drawing a garden rake. He progresses away from us narrowing the mess.

Robert is busy scrubbing graffiti from the wall in the bog.

He comes out of the cubicle carrying his bucket and disappears inside another.

Jamie is on his final round. He disappears round the top of the billet. The surrounds look immaculate and tidy, until

Out of the sand comes a camel spider.

It wanders off leaving a trail through the bands.

Jamie, a not too happy face, leaning on his hand.

He is sitting at a table in the mess. He is staring mournfully at a kipper on his plate. Just then a bright and breezy Robert comes.

ROBERT Wotcha.

He sits down, fetching his plate.

On the tannoy, a woman's yearning voice is singing a song.

ROBERT Why aren't you eating?

JAMIE It's all bones.

The helping hand of friendship: learning to bone a kipper

ROBERT All kippers have bones. There is a way of coping.

He reflects on the situation for a moment, then he says at a more intimate level

ROBERT Don't you know how?

Jamie shrugs.

ROBERT Would you like me to show you?

Jamie stops leaning on the table. He inclines himself round to suggest that he is taking up the offer. Robert sets about his own kipper.

ROBERT You set about it like so.

He frees the entire back bone with a slice of the knife and sets it neatly aside.

ROBERT It's easy when you know how to get rid of the rubbish. Try it.

Jamie fumbles away for a bit but gives up.

Robert switches their plates. Jamie whispers

JAMIE Thanks.

Robert shrugs. Then there is just the two of them quietly eating.

They wander along the sand between the two billets, a feeling of total lethargy in the air. It is reflected in the way Jamie is measuring the sand with his feet and in the kind of dislocated way Robert is moving. And this is how they are, one stopping, the other starting, sometimes separate, sometimes together, walking, standing.

Finally, the two of them are just standing there. Robert is gazing off in one direction, Jamie off in another. In a little while, unbeknown to Robert, Jamie will look at him, perhaps really studying him for the first time, then away again to appear as if he was thinking about something else. And eventually, Robert will do the same with Jamie, only this time Jamie will feel the look and turn. And they will both express the hint of a smile before turning away again to look at the sand.

Suddenly, Robert is pelting down the sand like some maniac let loose.

ROBERT Watch out!

He swiftly approaches Jamie, who is in position for leap-frog and flattens him to a heap. Robert laughs and his laughter is a kind of helpless thing as if he knows life to be the most marvellous thing. Suddenly, he springs to his feet, gathering Jamie.

ROBERT Come on, be alive, be alive, be alive, be alive!

He swings Jamie like a merry-go-round.

ROBERT This'll put some life into you.

With that he dumps him.

ROBERT Can't catch me.

But Jamie is immediately up and away in pursuit of

The zig-zagging Robert. And there they are for all the world like two kids at the seaside.

ROBERT He's alive, He IS alive!

Robert is lying on the sand, reading a book. Jamie is doing nothing, just lying flat on his back. He breaks the silence with

JAMIE I don't think I like people.

Robert finishes his sentence before looking up. He goes back to his book.

ROBERT Thanks.

Jamie glances round at Robert.

JAMIE I don't mean you.

He turns back to consider the sky again.

ROBERT Well, that's nice to know.

He reads for a bit, then turns to study Jamie.

ROBERT Anyway, people are alright.

JAMIE I want to do something.

Robert sighs, closes the book, tosses it down.

They are walking along the sand close to the barbed wire. Robert is seen to be lagging behind. He looks remarkably bored, sauntering here, sauntering there. Then he takes up a stance to watch Jamie, who has meanwhile turned to watch him. They are like statues.

Robert raises his arm and lets it flag against his thigh in an effort to express his feelings about the aimlessness of it all.

Jamie turns aimlessly away.

Robert crouches to the sand to watch

An insect slowly wending its way.

It is while he is watching this that the sound of the plane comes. He rises to listen to the engine revving up, then the sound of it like a long-held sigh.

Then the charge of it along the runway and into the sky, disappearing.

Robert watches long after it has gone. Then, moving off,

He confronts the waiting Jamie.

ROBERT C'mon, you. I thought we were going to be doing something.

No reaction from Jamie. Robert looks irritable.

ROBERT Come on!

JAMIE Don't you like walking?

ROBERT We've walked.

Jamie thinks.

JAMIE Well, let's talk then.

ROBERT What about if it isn't you?

There is a hint of a smile on Jamie's face.

JAMIE Well, let's go to the pictures then.

ROBERT We've seen it.

Silence. Robert now gives up, turns away, disappears. Jamie follows.

They are walking along behind the barbed wire. Robert turns to walk backwards. When finally he stops, Jamie stops.

ROBERT C'mon now, what we want is one constructive idea.

JAMIE Can you think of something?

ROBERT No, it should come from you for a change.

But nothing comes.

Robert begins to back away.

ROBERT Look, I'll see you later, okay?

With that he turns and goes.

Jamie is at his bed space in the billet. His open locker door has pictures of Marilyn Monroe hanging on it. He rummages inside for his uniform.

The fans on the ceiling are making whirring sounds in an otherwise silent place.

Robert is sitting on the edge of a bed putting Duraglit to his buttons. This is his space in the billet. On the wall surrounding him – he occupies a corner bed – hang pictures of Eisenstein and Sibelius. There is also a picture of a skull divided up into different compartments like rooms in a house. His bedside table is piled with books. Jamie dumps his uniform on the bed and sits down beside him. Then he turns his gaze to the pile of books and says

JAMIE What a lot of books you've got.

Robert doesn't look up, just answers

ROBERT I've got a lot more at home.

Jamie takes one of the books, turns it about for a bit and puts it back.

Robert hands the jacket over to Jamie, who proceeds to wipe off the Duraglit. They remain in silence just cleaning away.

Robert is lying on the sand on his back, this time reading another book. Jamie is again sitting there doing nothing. He looks bored. He shovels up a handful of sand and lets it slip through his fingers. He glances at Robert but there is nothing going there. He lies back on the sand but a moment later is shooting up again. He sighs. His voice when it comes seems to ache from boredom.

JAMIE Do you want to do something?

Robert, an enclosed isolated face lost in his reading. He lets out a brief laugh, then is silent again.

JAMIE I'm bored.

Robert finishes his sentence before looking up. He considers Jamie for a moment then turns on his side. He moves his index finger to make a small cross in the sand.

ROBERT Do you know what that is?

Jamie, an isolated face. He looks puzzled.

ROBERT That's you.

He pauses to let that sink in. Then he forms another cross about a foot distant.

ROBERT That's me.

Robert's finger moves with forceful deliberation to draw a line separating the two crosses.

Then picking up his book he goes.

He crosses the sand, goes inside the billet, lets the door go.

Jamie, an isolated figure, watching.

Inside, Robert is lying quite still on his bed with his hands clasped together across his forehead, not a particularly happy face.

From the back of a jeep, we pass beside the line of painted bricks and out through the main gates where a large sign announces 'Royal Air Force Abu Sueir'.

Jamie is a solitary figure in the back of the jeep, his body juddering in rhythm to the

Sound of the engine.

The rhythm changes

As the vehicle takes a curve into the town square and screeches to a halt.

The cabin door slams shut, then there is a hint of the driver disappearing swiftly through a swing door.

Jamie, a huddled sleeping face. He raises his hand to rub his eye with the back of his hand, the way a child does, then he lowers it to rest on his rifle.

Sound of a child's voice pleading pathetically

BOY Faloos?

But Jamie is lost in the land of nod.

The voice comes again, a little more prominent

BOY Kateer faloos.

Jamie opens his eyes on

A child in rags. He has his hand raised up. Now he moves it to his mouth to suggest taking in food. Then he picks up his vest to rub his stomach and back to his mouth again, before reaching up.

Jamie makes a hopeless gesture suggesting he hasn't got anything. He hears the boy say

BOY Money.

The boy simply extends his hand more.

Jamie has the insides of his pockets held out.

JAMIE I'm sorry, I've no money.

A mother and child in a hut like something out of a nativity.

Sounds of the engine revving up.

The boy's face breaks into a glorious smile and the once pleading hand becomes something that waves.

The vehicle draws Jamie away and he too is smiling and waving.

The boy becomes a small figure still waving.

The vehicle carrying Jamie looks small and insignificant. The landscape it is passing through is undisturbed except for a long single track as if left there by a phantom wheel. The jeep reaches the line, runs parallel with it for a time, then breaks through.

There is a group huddled in a circle in the middle of the billet floor.

In the centre, amongst the knees and plimsoles, there is a wriggling camel spider. A hand fetches a tin of paraffin and proceeds to pour a generous supply of liquid round the creature.

Jamie, a passive face, watching.

Another hand strikes a match, lowers it, leaves it suspended.

Jamie breaks away from the circle with its private ritual, and

Goes to join up with Robert, who is quietly ruling out a chart. When finally the private circle lets out a victorious yell and stampedes and slams the door, it is Robert who looks up. He goes back to his task. Then Jamie looks up.

JAMIE Can I borrow one of your books?

Robert doesn't bother to look up this time.

ROBERT Help yourself.

Jamie picks up a book, opens it.

JAMIE Thanks.

He wanders off. Robert watches after him. Then he considers his chart. After the words TIME EX it has been blocked off into days. At the tail end it says HOME. His hand comes to fill in another box,

Then he turns to pin it up on the wall.

Jamie, turned away on his bed, enclosed, reading the book.

The spider is a charred mess on the floor.

JAMIE What're you doing?

He approaches Robert carrying yet another book in his hand. He sits on a ridge of sand. Robert has a pen poised in his hand.

ROBERT Writing home.

He gives up, groans.

ROBERT I can't think of anything to say. You're lucky.

Previous page: Jamie takes the initiative: with Robert in Cairo

JAMIE Why?

ROBERT You don't have that problem.

Jamie thinks about it.

JAMIE I wouldn't mind.

Robert plonks the pad and pen on Jamie's lap.

ROBERT Go on then, you write something.

Jamie puts the pad right back where it came from.

JAMIE I don't know your family.

ROBERT Well, now's your chance.

He rips a sheet from the pad, makes Jamie take it. Then he is content to let the sand drift through his fingers.

Jamie begins to write a line or two. Then

JAMIE How many L's are there in 'wonderful'? One or two?

Jamie comes yelling down the sand. He has a bayonet in his grasp.

He thrusts it into a sawdust bag.

They are waiting outside the cinema next to the sign 'Q Here'.

They are in their usual manner of distraction. Jamie barely steals a glance at the not so oblivious Robert, but he in turn manages to study the other quite hard.

We hear a plane taking off overhead.

Jamie asks into space

JAMIE What will you do when you get back?

ROBERT I suppose I'll eventually go to university.

He turns.

ROBERT How about you?

JAMIE I want to be an artist.

He turns to look

At a poster for *Niagara*.

He thinks hard for a moment. Then he turns adding

JAMIE Maybe even a film director.

Robert's voice is a curious mixture of suspended belief and release at hearing something positive.

ROBERT Wow!

Robert focuses his camera.

ROBERT Say 'cheese'.

Jamie is posing in a galabea.

ROBERT Smile!

And, we feel for the first time ever, Jamie smiles.

Cairo. At a table outside a coffee shop, Jamie and Robert are relaxing. An Arab boy brings Jamie a hookah and sets it up for him.

JAMIE Thank you.

Robert watches as Jamie tries this new experience.

Later, the city street is full of activity

My Way Home: Jamie packs his kit bag

Except for Robert and Jamie who are just standing around.

ROBERT Okay, what shall we do now?

JAMIE I know a place we could go.

He fetches out a guide-book from his pocket, glances through it. Now he opens up the map to study that. During this, Robert is looking at Jamie in an amused way as much as to say, well, look at him! Jamie manoeuvres the map to get his bearings right.

Then he traces his finger along the route.

The place of interest is a mosque and there are many people going towards it, removing their shoes before they enter.

We hear the mullah calling.

Robert and Jamie come in to look around. They are separate for a moment, Jamie engrossed in his guide book. Then Jamie comes to pull Robert.

JAMIE Hey, Robert. Look.

He points up.

They are small figures now against the mosaic. Merely a detail at first, it gradually opens up to become an all-enveloping complete thing.

Jamie is quietly packing his kit bag. He goes to his locker door where he screws up the Marilyn pin-ups but retains and pockets the last one. Then he looks off and he doesn't look too happy.

Robert is busy putting finishing touches to a map. Jamie dumps his bag and sits down.

ROBERT Look, here's the way to get there.

He hands it to Jamie.

ROBERT Put it in a safe place.

Jamie, an isolated face, studying the map.

ROBERT If you feel like it, look us up sometime. There's no need to be shy.

He can hear Robert add

ROBERT If you like, you can stay.

Then

ROBERT If you want, you can call it home.

Then the sounds of things drift away and it is as if Jamie is deep inside himself.

Deep inside his mind's eye he is seeing the place of his childhood. It comes to him first as a small white abstraction of things, then a gradual opening out to something all-embracing.

And there is a sound that comes with it, growing, a gathering up like a long sigh. The sound extends itself towards the window, becomes that of a plane taking off.

Beyond the window there is an orchard in full bloom. And the sun is a promising thing.

In flight the sound remains constant for a while before dying to nothing,

Save for the hint of a homely dog, alive with it, barking.

A life finally blossoms

In 1976, flying south, Bill Douglas looked forward optimistically to shooting the second, Egyptian part of *My Way Home*. During the flight he held the hands of Judy Cottam, his producer, since flying was her sole identified fear. She would need her courage in days to come. Changes in climate, circumstances, the very substance of his story would, Douglas believed, make him a reformed directorial character:

> I took stock of the situation. I had a lot to be grateful for. I had completed half the film's shooting (the previous year). The first part had taken place in Scotland. I had survived that dark journey, the re-enactment of my youth, and now I was coming out into the Egyptian light. I felt good. I was going to film a friendship. I was about to pay homage to the person who had helped me grow.
>
> And I was going to be very nice. I was going to dispel the reputation I had for being difficult. What was it that made me such a monster? Could it be that it was painful resurrecting old memories? Or was it not having enough money or time to shoot? Well, all that was in the past now. I had done my homework super plus. I would stick rigidly with the set-ups (98 in all) and dialogue as planned in the script. What was there to get het up about? Ten shots a day seemed like luxury and we would even have the weekend free. Enthusiasm, that's all I needed behind me. Yes, the angel in me was about to emerge.

> **Yes, I can be very difficult. Lots of people say it so I'll agree that I can be difficult.**
>
> BILL DOUGLAS

As we shall see, what actually happened in Egypt would have broken the patience of a saint, let alone an aspirant Scottish angel. For good reason and ill, the redemption of a difficult reputation was not to be won on foreign soil. Certainly, difficulty in film-making was not that to which Douglas aspired. Joan Littlewood's ensemble playing as a model of creative collaboration remained his ideal. Asked by Charles Rees in 1978 whether he would have preferred to do everything on his own in making his films, he replied:

> Absolutely not. I couldn't do everything. I don't want to be a cameraman. I just want to write the script and to make the film. Like Littlewood, if you like, I like ensemble playing. *We* are making the film. The best moments in

film to me, certainly in my experience, are the ones where we were working together to do something.

Among his scribbled notes other aspirations to group virtue have turned up:

> A film is a little world in itself. When you carry a film, you carry the weight of it on your shoulders. If the director is like Atlas, this is okay. Now I never set out to take the whole load of anything in life. After all we are supposed to be in this together. Same with film. In the beginning I said 'we' not 'I'. And I asked for suggestions.
>
> Unfortunately not everyone feels the same way. Far from it. One day I complained about somebody not bothering and I got the reply, 'Well, you're getting a film out of it.' This attitude prevailed throughout the three films. A director is by nature alone with his creation. He can't escape that. If he is not prepared for almost total isolation it can be a frightening thing. Then he will really come to know what sleepless nights are. He will develop an anxious look. And when he comes to show concern for his film, for this weight he carries, they will christen him not Atlas but paranoid.

Douglas was deeply unfair about much of the co-operation he received in making the *Trilogy*. Partly by apparent coincidence but mainly by design of Mamoun Hasan, Head of Production at the BFI for the first two parts of the *Trilogy*, Douglas was aided on production, camera and editing by some young, raw but exceptionally talented and committed people, as many of their subsequent careers testify. They realised that something of extraordinary cinematic importance was taking place. Most testify to it as a period of singular growth in their understanding of the medium and the development of their own talent. In an industry noted for the shoot as being a discrete event with a subsequent dispersal of personnel, it has been remarked that many of the people involved in the *Trilogy* kept in touch. Though he did not seem to realise it at the time, Douglas did create a community of fellow spirits.

Much of the difficulty also stemmed from external forces acting on him. Implicit in cinema is the difficulty caused by the relationship of money to time. Douglas's film-making was always chronically under-resourced. The three parts of the BFI-funded *Trilogy* were made for slightly in excess of £3,000, £12,000 and £33,000 respectively. Douglas had to make two trips back to Scotland with Mick Campbell and Gale Tattersall respectively in order to complete *My Child-hood* because the original shoot had simply run out of money. Egypt was an even greater financial nightmare. Of this shoot Douglas wrote:

> I was very difficult and I realised that it was to do with having very little money, very little time, and trying to bring the film in on schedule. And I had to do a lot of shouting. I had to keep the thing moving. Otherwise I would never have done it. . . . It's very difficult. . . . It's to do with pressure, there's a lot of pressure in getting the film done in such short time. I mean, d'you know the whole Egyptian sequence, which lasts about half an hour. . . . How long do you think I had to shoot? That's a half-hour film. I had eight days. Eight days. . . . I was rushing all the time, running and rushing, and it was very tiring. You have to concentrate on little details or you can miss them from being in a hurry. I always want to be economical. I'm not complaining about the small amount of money, I really like to work with a small amount of money.

To these financial issues, there has to be added Douglas's internal pain and turmoil as he cinematically recreated his own savage childhood. Douglas tended to be ambivalent about the relationship of his own behaviour on the set and the content of his story. At times he would deny any relationship. On other occasions he would admit to it being partly true:

> . . . the reason why I was very difficult was because I was dealing, at times, with very painful aspects of my childhood. And it was very unnerving to deal with some of the little areas that had caused a great deal of pain. So that I wasn't really – at times of setting these scenes up, using the boy I brought into the film to re-enact some terrible happenings – at that time I wasn't the nicest person to come and ask anything. It used to bother me a great deal.

Not only was Douglas summoning up such monsters from the deep but he was doing it in the very village a quarter century after the actual events so that many of the witnesses of the events were still there. This was provocative of mutual unease, if not suspicion. At best, he abandoned his mainly English crew to their own devices. He was a man alone between worlds, relating neither to the village nor to his fellow film-makers. The locations for shooting the *Trilogy*, then, were pressure chambers filled with the turbulence of psychological, fiscal, technical, familial, social, bureaucratic and ethnic forces. It was an explosive mix, and explosions there were. Tantrums and objects were thrown by Douglas. Some people cracked under the pressure and a few others were sacked. Generally the atmosphere was one of fraught, painful, obsessive intensity. It was often hard to distinguish apparently gratuitous cruelty in Douglas's behaviour from the fact that he would go to any lengths to achieve exactly his conception of what should be on camera. On other occasions, as Brand Thumin, Douglas's editor on *My Childhood*, records, there was no doubt that a dark, compulsive streak emerged, only capriciously related to the task in hand.

> While I know all his good points outside film-making, Bill could be very difficult. There were times in his career when he was really taking it out on people around him; he was definitely ill-treating people. I like, admire and respect Bill but I refuse to say that wasn't the case because it is very rare that you have somebody who is so ill-treated themselves who is not going to ill-treat somebody in their own adult life. Bill wasn't a saint, he was a human being and he did do that. When he did it, it was terrible. He would make you feel that you were not three-dimensional; you felt that you were a cardboard cut-out. From a dark early life, it is a cliché, people do take it out later on those closest to them. Film-making involves a temporary family or group life with that degree of intimacy and possibility of giving hurt.

Others have spoken of Douglas's ability to intimidate. Mamoun Hassan believes a pattern, of which Douglas himself was not aware, was discernible in his generation of unholy terror.

> Somebody had to be kicked off the picture. They had to leave because they could not take it, and only then would Bill feel that the poison had gone out of the shoot. I do not know what the psychological reason for it was, and it does not matter, but he needed a sacrificial person. Once the person was sacked, there was a dramatic transformation in Bill's behaviour. I thought in *My Childhood* that the particular person was simply in his way, but he used to load that person with so much, as it were, malice and evil that on the second occasion one realised that someone had to be sacrificed. It was a tendency in Bill that he needed someone to carry evil out of his film.

If Douglas subconsciously was satisfied that evil was banished from the set, the general testimony is that suffering certainly was not. Hassan, because of his acuity and a degree of detachment from the actual fraught process, describes the environment thus:

He made people work for him through pain. I mean that literally. I've never seen people more unhappy than on a Bill Douglas shoot. He made people do what he wanted them to by, as it were, connecting with depression. Everybody became very, very depressed on his films, but it was a radically different kind of depression because in normal depressions people under-achieve whereas here they over-achieved. They did their best work for him. Maybe it was not depression but grief; he made everyone connect with their grief so that there was no kind of joy in the making of his films. There was the most curious atmosphere, which I have never seen before or after. Nor did Bill consciously know what he was doing because it was too intuitive and too effective. I remember Peter Harvey, the soundman, saying, 'I could flatten him with one punch but he terrified the life out of me.' The terror he imposed on everybody was at root the terror of themselves, of some kind of deep buried childhood emotion, because the thing that Bill did, in an extraordinarily brave, heroic way, was to connect with his own primal grief. Also, Bill never subjected anybody to more than he subjected himself. He did it the only way he knew how and managed to get a continuity of vision from shot to shot with people who were inexperienced, not paid properly and working under conditions of tremendous physical and material difficulty. To be able to achieve that singular vision and that consistent style from shot to shot was amazing; people don't realise this because once you achieve something everything looks easy, inevitable.

Hassan was also aware that the fraught intensity of effort which took place behind the camera had been preceded by the solitary but no less intense effort of Douglas's writing methods. In his invaluable 1978 discussion with Charles Rees and Hassan, Douglas did talk about this to – for him – an unusual degree. He had a self-preserving principle not to let the explanatory intrude into the realm of his creativity. Hence, too, his refusal to read any criticism of his films whether eulogistic or belittling. Asked if he felt he had a special gift for dialogue, Douglas responded:

I don't know that I have a gift for dialogue. The dialogue in the films really emerges for me out of writing the scene. And I don't really plan ahead what I'm going to write. I put the blank paper in the typewriter and write the scene and the dialogue and the atmosphere and the scene takes over, sort of thing, and the dialogue will emerge out of that. And it'll feel true to me or not. And on a subsequent draft – there's usually about two or three –

usually about the third one, it's done. And they'll sort of be wiped out or remain in. I just go on whether I believe it or not. . . . I do a first draft and I work it straight through to the end. Then it grows, and the third time it's the same procedure until I feel that I have reached the whole idea . . . I usually work for long hours straight through so as I can keep in touch with what I wrote on page one and that it has some meaning to me when I'm on page thirty, if you like, otherwise you can lose the threads. And you have to try to keep a hold of the whole conception of the thing. So that's my method of starting at nine o'clock in the morning and going right through. I mean, I can go through till six and forget to take a cup of tea . . . or eat something, to keep a hold of it. . . . Maybe it's knowing that I will sometimes get stuck, I don't put any full-stops. I always put commas. If I put a full-stop, I always feel that it isn't, I'm going to go on, you see.

Rees and Hassan were painfully aware of the enormous aesthetic problem of translating such an intensely wrought, fluidly envisioned script into film. Rees elicited the following response from Douglas on this crucial issue, the issue which is the real root of Douglas's capacity for being difficult, and of his genius:

When I'm writing the script, say, and I'm dealing with a scene between characters, I go through . . . I'm actually in it. So I go through that kind of thing with it. . . . Sometimes I wander through the flat and I'm sort of totally lost in it . . . I'm totally inside the thing. I hope that when it's actually being filmed, it's going through the celluloid, that same thing is recaptured for me. And when it's going through the editing, away from location, here we are sitting at this, the editor and I, and it's going through the feeling. I always rely on the feelings coming back again. If they're true, you know. So maybe, maybe if it is difficult to communicate, it's that.

This is an area of inevitable, horrendous difficulty. For Douglas, the recreation of memory was not simply accuracy of factual recall. His interpretation of Chekhov's concept of memory as a filter had a continued, special importance for him.

Well, when, say, I'm writing a scene with my grandfather sitting at a table or whatever it is, if it's going to work for me, the scene, the writing, I'm totally within the atmosphere of the room. Even when I'm down here. . . . I know where I come from and I carry that with me. I haven't stopped being a Scot because I came to live in London. And all the atmospheres, the sensations and the smells of things, remain with me. And when I'm trying to recapture the impression of something – the atmosphere of the room – the smell of it comes back to me. And when I see the man there who is going to be my grandfather, I will hypnotise him into being that thing. And he sits there, and I come and we look through the camera and I'm looking again for these sensations I felt when I was writing. Maybe I will it into there, I don't know, but I believe it when I'm looking through the camera at that set-up, and I know what you like – you don't want me shooting all over the place, you want me to be decisive, and I like that I've made a decision, that it is absolutely right that it starts with a close-up and then it's a long shot and it ends with somebody going out and closing the door, you see, and the held atmosphere. So that I'm just recapturing what I truly felt at the time – I laughed here when I was doing it, and when there was crying, I cried here when I was doing it – I really went through it all. I'm all the characters, if you like, and one is really putting that back again. And if I don't feel it, then I know it's a lie for me. And when we are in the editing, hopefully one is bringing that back.

By definition, the film set does not provide the tranquillity for recollecting such emotions or, indeed, for testing the quality of what has been filmed against them. Even the quieter, more intimate editing room was to pose dire problems in relationships. The intensity of Douglas's empathy for his recreated characters perhaps led, with its own logic, to an apparent hard indifference to the crew around him. For personal reasons and, more important, for practical functioning, he could not possibly communicate the level of his emotional arousal. Hassan, aware of the particular problem, suggested that in all writer-directors there tended, on one side or another, to be an imbalance between their subjective talent for writing and their objective capacity for the actual act of filming. Douglas's reply was deeply revealing with regard to the ideal relationship he conceived of as possible in film-making and his own occasional ability to achieve such conditions of working empathy. In this, as in so many other respects, Douglas's utopian vision was a silent one.

I must say it varied with different people I was relating to and they were mostly behind the scenes. For instance, I think I'm right in saying, when I was working with Gale Tattersall, I honestly didn't feel that I had to say very much. I never found that I was being questioned about why we were doing this ... what did this mean ... anything like that. It was to do with the practical thing of setting up the camera, of going up on the roof, of looking down on things, or a discussion simply about the framing of something. And what one was trying to get at. I never felt the pressure there at all. I agree that sometimes if a person wants to know an awful lot, then one is going into the territory of trying to explain and it's as difficult as trying to explain to you now. I don't know what the meaning of things are. I have no idea what things mean. I just work the script, and there's a beginning, there's a middle and an end; and I know of echoes that are happening here and there. Someone might say, 'Well, you must have seen that, what that meant.' But I didn't. And it's that silence that one is allowed to maintain with people that helps enormously when one just goes and takes it.'

The *Trilogy* could not have been created without the men and women who did follow Douglas's lead. Their altruism and talent more than compensated for their lack of experience. In any case, both in acting and technical work, Douglas preferred the amateur to the professional. This was another cause of tension. As Douglas told Rees:

Well, there is a very definite difference between actors and non-actors. I think the more successful the actor becomes, the more removed he looks, somehow. There's something terribly smooth about him and terribly sort of well-slept and well-looked after, some sort of look about them, their faces. And you look at a person who just lives life and they're far more interesting to look at, I think. They seem to have the problems of life on their faces, you know. Not that I necessarily want them to have the problems of life on their face, but life seems to leave its marks, and they don't seem to be over-concerned about … removing them, or covering it. And maybe the actor covers. You've got to go inside, underneath with an actor, I think.

Douglas preferred non-professional actors who would, with naked faces, act out discrete scenes and were not concerned with knowing the whole plot so that they might create an independent meaningful performance for themselves and thereby distort the director's creation of the film as open, ambivalent, unwinding. To place professional, theatrically trained actors in such a context was, of course, to create frictive anxiety. As Douglas commented:

The only difficulty with actors was that you had to get them to trust you. I find that non-actors trust you immediately. And I find actors worry terribly if you don't give them the script to read. They like to read a script and they like to formulate their character. And if they don't have that something to hang on to, they're terribly insecure, you know. Some would be actually slipping behind my back and nosing in somebody's script, so I had little bits of struggle, and once I actually got them to see that they should try to trust me, that I wasn't going to try to make a fool of them, I certainly wouldn't try to do it to anybody, but once I actually got them to see that ... I think I even went so far as saying, 'If you don't like the rushes, if you don't like what you see, I won't use it.' In fact, having done that, you got their trust and you knew that they were never going to ask you. And it went on okay after that.

The actor whose face and soul dominate the *Trilogy* was the least professional of people. Douglas's hunch that this silent, evasive child was absolutely right was perhaps his most inspired. Stephen Archibald gave him what he hoped for from everybody on set:

Well, Stephen was very like me. I mean his quietness was the ... quietness and introspection I once had, and I think I still have a bit. ... He didn't need very much to be explained. I mean sometimes I'd go up to him and I'd say,

Bill meeting Stephen at Heathrow airport, 1973

'Stephen, I would like you to go over there and actually do this or that', and I'd look at his eye, and I could see that he knew exactly what I was talking about. I'd just glance at him and say, 'Oh, you know what I mean.' And I knew exactly he knew. It was as if he was my left arm. It was very peculiar but this happened so many times. ... And yet he never read the script, because I never give the script to anybody to read if I can get away with it. Sometimes it's a bit of a struggle. But I certainly didn't with Stephen because he doesn't know how to read a film script. He always just gave me the impression that he knew what he was doing. And I left him pretty free.

MY CHILDHOOD

During his year at the London Film School, Douglas became 'increasingly obsessed' with making a film about his own childhood. He was helped in this by discussing the project with his admired tutor, Michael Truman. Indeed, the original script, involving a story in flashback in which the main character, Jimmy, returns to the village of his childhood where he had been known as Jamie, was written as an element of the school's diploma requirement. Douglas then gave this script to Lindsay Anderson who, to Douglas's great consternation, immediately intuited that it was autobiographical. Anderson also suggested dropping the film's flashback formula and its evasive title and calling it simply *My Childhood*. Douglas also found very helpful Anderson's probing questions about the shoot when he actually started to set up camera positions.

Seeking finance rather than creative help produced more ambivalent results. Films of Scotland's then director, Forsyth Hardy, replied:

I am returning to you the script you left with me for *Jamie*. I have read it with interest. It certainly suggests a nostalgic film about a bit of Scotland which is disappearing. I hope the BFI confirm their support for you. It is only fair to say without delay that it is not a subject in which the Films of Scotland Committee would be interested. One of our main concerns is to project a forward-looking country and although it is no criticism of the film as a film – this would not do so.

Fortunately, the BFI did confirm support. This coincided with Bruce Beresford leaving the BFI as Head of Production and his replacement by Mamoun Hassan. Douglas thought his script had been rejected by Beresford; what is certain is that

Mamoun Hassan discovered it among a pile on the desk. On reading it he was instantly aware of a genuine cinematic imagination, a visual poet who, in Hassan's definition, did not conventionally film action but made manifest 'the shot of the thing itself, a shot which cannot be taken from any other angle'. Or, as Douglas would say, 'Every shot is a verb.' To corroborate his reading, Hassan screened Douglas's student film *Come Dancing*. He found the evidence overwhelming. The committee passed script and budget. Douglas was given the maximum grant of £150. 'You'll make an important film. I know it,' Hassan wrote to him. One condition the committee laid down was, however, less propitious. To have any commercial viability, they felt, it had to be a colour film. To make the best of a bad artistic judgment, Douglas thought that the tension between colour and content might be turned to aesthetic advantage. Thus the film was shot in colour. When the rushes came in, however, Hassan decided, in the name of cheapness, to have them printed in black and white. When the rushes were screened, the evidence of the aesthetic rightness of this decision was so overwhelming that any notion of colour printing was immediately dropped.

When in Glasgow, Douglas, prompted by Eddie Dick, started to write a memoir of the making of the *Trilogy*. For various reasons, mainly his desire to be creating not remembering, his heart was unfortunately not in it. This brief piece shows what might have been, and also finely illuminates the period just prior to shooting.

I have to move fast. Surveyors advise the villagers be rehoused. Due to instability of the mine seams running directly underneath, the village is slipping. Within weeks the villagers are packing their bags. I am surprised to discover how many are leaving all their furniture behind. I feel like a thief wandering at will from house to house through other people's belongings. It isn't difficult to go inside for the doors are unlocked and many open to the skies. As poor as these people are, there are treasures to be found, no doubt sentimental reminders of great-grandparents long since gone. Here a large silver frame, there one of the earliest (Kodak) cameras or a simple Victorian child's hoop. On a more personal level, I find an army registration card replete with identity snapshot. I remember the man. He must be a pensioner now. During World War II he is called abroad leaving a wife and son who is in my class at school. His mother abandons him for another part of Scotland and another man. She doesn't return. There are no treasures here, only reminders of a hard bachelor existence. I seek out the son and discover his father has not survived the sudden upheaval. I ask him if he wouldn't like a reminder of his father. It appears they were estranged some time before. Soon the bulldozers will arrive to churn all into rubble. But not before the real thieves come from outside to plunder.

In the nick of time the British Film Institute give me the backing for *My Childhood*. Three thousand pounds, shooting on sixteen-millimetre in black and white. I sign the contract in January for shooting in September, the best month for the best light in Scotland. By the time September comes, three-quarters of the village is deserted. The soundman is happy for the silence. The villages have been swallowed into nearby Craigmillar, the home of the plunderers of their belongings. During the three weeks' shoot the soundman is due for a heart attack. The bulldozers are moving in. Then a word with the labourers has them generously working hand in hand.

As well as BFI backing there was another major piece of good fortune in this period. Douglas had been sitting in Moultrie Kelsall's coffee-house, 'The Laigh', unaware of who the owner was or that he kept hovering around the table listening to Douglas's evidently lucid sketches of the actors he wanted for various roles. Kelsall revealed his identity and told Douglas that he knew several appropriate people. From this chance conversation came Jean Taylor Smith, Helena Gloag, Paul Kermack, Anne Smith and Eileen MacCallum. Eileen MacCallum remembers being approached by Kelsall, who told her that there was little or no money in the work but he felt it was deeply important. Though Douglas, in some instances, had initial misgivings about theatrically derived style, and indeed took on professional actors because 'he was rushed for time', he was grateful for the speed with which they tuned into his sparse, minimalist acting style. Though some of them had severe misgivings at first about the milieu of the story (Jean Taylor Smith is reported as being discovered off camera trying to give Stephen Archibald and Hughie Restorick elocution lessons) and the requirement to perform discrete, near-improvisations rather than theatre's 'complete', self-conceived roles, they all quickly realised that Douglas was to be trusted to create a cinematic whole of which they were quite excellent organic parts. With actors, his own instincts and Joan Littlewood's education rarely failed him.

Casting his amateur actors was also not without strange coincidence. Douglas spent weeks looking for his two boys. In the end, they found him. Two truants, Stephen Archibald and Hughie Restorick, approached Douglas standing at a bus shelter. Douglas records the encounter thus:

I was going to a school. There are many schools in Edinburgh but I chose the one nearest to my village, and I was sitting in Edinburgh at the time waiting for a bus to take me down there. And there were two boys playing truant. They were friends. They came along the street and I was smoking a cigarette and the elder one said to me, 'Can I have a drag on your fag, mister?' And I said, 'I'm sorry but you're far too young.' I didn't ask them to stay, I was completely preoccupied with finding those children. And I was looking frightfully smart because I was meeting the headmaster and I thought I'd better give him a good impression, you know, small budget or no. And I'm looking for boys for a film.

And those two boys sat down and the little one who played me was very quiet and the other one just kept chatting away with me. And I thought – I kept answering their questions – and then I suddenly realised that there they were, and I needn't go any further. And I said to them, 'Would you like to be in a film?' 'What's the story about?' And I said, 'Oh, never mind the story.' 'How much do we get?' And I said, just off the top of my head, 'Well, four pounds.' And of course they nearly leapt into the busy thoroughfare at this fortune they were going to get. I asked them for their names and addresses and took it down, and I thought, well, that's it, you know, they're boys and I'll never see them again. And they went off and they disappeared

Passport photos of Stephen Archibald and Hugh Restorick after their first encounter with Bill Douglas, 1971

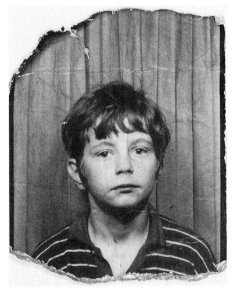 

round the corner and I thought, 'Oh gosh, I know they don't want to be in a film.'

The children, however, did want to be in a film and, though tracking them down was to be deeply problematic, especially since Archibald had given Douglas a false address, they were, much against school and local judgment, confirmed in their roles. Their headmaster was particularly opposed. For him, the school was filled with much more talented, deserving cases, and he insisted that when not filming the miscreants should be safely in their classroom. Of the headmaster, Douglas wrote:

> Needless to say, our relationship was strained from the start. He had reluctantly agreed to let me have the two boys for two days only in each of the three weeks. Naturally I had worried how I was going to get a performance out of them in the time. The boys themselves solved the problem. They wanted to film. They did not want to go to school. And nothing I or anyone else could do could move them to the contrary. It was true the headmaster's negation of them was positive for me. I was finding them intelligent, highly imaginative, and helpful. And never truants. In fact, so engrossed were they that I had difficulty making them go home at the day's end. Seeing the children visibly improving themselves, I chose to break the law. As luck would have it, it wasn't until the final day of shooting when the headmaster sent the law in my direction.

Never an ideologue, Douglas did have an anti-authoritarian politics of creativity. On bitter personal experience, he saw underprivilege as not only material but imaginative deprivation. Given a chance, all sorts of entombed talents, he believed, could be resurrected. Though he rather tended to rub his English professional crew's noses in it, he did recruit some astonishing local talent.

> I set about finding my cast: non-actors – or actors if I was short of time. Usually they found me – such as the two boys when they were playing truant from school; or were brought to me by others – such as the owner of the hotel who, on overhearing me on the telephone describing a character, furnished her as soon as I replaced the receiver. She was employed behind the bar! On yet another occasion, exactly one day prior to shooting a particular scene (in *My Ain Folk*), I mentioned out loud not having found my soldier. The mother of one of the boys, who was dressing the set (Elsie

Restorick), asked me to describe the soldier. She looked as delighted as a child finding sixpence in a Christmas cake. 'You've seen him, Bill.' She drove me to a place where I could see him again. It was the man who had supplied me with second-hand furniture. Oddly enough it always seemed that people sensed correctly what I needed.

The prodigal's return to actually make the film was inauspicious. Ben MacKenna, Douglas's half-brother/cousin, answered the door on a wet September evening to discover Douglas, unseen since the late 50s, soaked on the threshold. MacKenna took Douglas out the next morning to buy him new shoes to replace his badly holed ones. MacKenna, memorably, played his own father in the first two films. Another local pressed into service along with her husband, to play the teacher and janitor at the very beginning of *My Childhood*, was the remarkable Helen Crummy. She ran the local Craigmillar Festival for sixteen years with an extra-ordinary combination of warmth and political and creative idealism. She, with David Brown, the councillor for Craigmillar and Douglas's lifelong friend, provided him with indispensable links back into the world he wanted to film. Crummy's primary memory is how hard-up and hungry they all were. Endless tea was dispensed. Generally the villagers were very helpful. There was, however, some unease, apparently not so much about the particular tragedy of the Bever-idge girls as that the film might reveal to the world a poverty best hidden if not wholly forgotten or indeed escaped from. Douglas recalled:

> A solitary villager is concerned about me revealing poverty. She wants me to make a 'glamorous' film about village life, her adjective not mine. I warn the crew not to part with the script under any circumstances. I'm afraid if the word gets round how much poverty there will be in the finished film they might banish me.

Douglas devised not a few strategies throughout the shoot to hide what he was doing, though several of the older people had worrying glimpses of images of a past they thought best forgotten. Also, to be fair, their sense of the village as community was different from that of a marginalised, deprived child. Sadly, when they were taken to see it at its screening at the Edinburgh Film Festival their reaction was, at best, dismay:

> The villagers did take exception to the poverty depicted in the film. It wasn't my intention actually to make a thing out of the poverty. But it was a bit

difficult to avoid it since we were very poor. So it was there. But they saw that and they were a bit put out because I was going to be showing the film abroad. That bothered them a great deal, you see.

These were, literally, little local difficulties compared to the troubles that almost immediately blew up on set. The main issue was the first cameraman, Bahram Manocheri. A letter from Geoffrey Evans, in charge of production, to the BFI Production Board lists the problems. Manocheri had initially refused to work without certain pieces of equipment. After 'a particularly successful performance by the boy actor', it was found that the film had not been laced inside the camera. Manocheri criticised Stephen Archibald to the point of tears and flight. 'The director,' Evans reported with no trace of irony, 'showed great forbearance in not responding angrily to any of these events, which would have broken lesser men.' The breaking point was reached with the cameraman refusing to shoot in bright sunlight two short close-ups of Archibald. Evans reported:

> Bill Douglas finally snapped and agreed that he must have a new camera-man, whereupon he ordered Mr Manocheri off the picture.
>
> Within minutes all the tension appeared to have been removed and Bill Douglas and Bahram Manocheri appeared to have agreed as adults that they could not work together; indeed a perfectly affable discussion was held between myself and Bahram on the way to Waverley station, where it appeared that he would have been glad to leave earlier had he felt that a suitable replacement was available: one feels that this latter is scarcely his decision, and we now have a pragmatic, professional, experienced, hard-working lighting cameraman which is what the production needs to survive.

Mick Campbell, a more relaxed cameraman who had known Douglas at film school, took over. Until editing, Douglas did not realise that Campbell, when filming, had allowed the camera 'to breathe'; that is, in close-up he made tiny adjustments in relation to the subject. Indiscernible to the normal eye, this did not suit Douglas's desire for absolute stasis.

If the key problem of the cameraman was solved, other problems, to become exacerbated on subsequent shoots, manifested themselves. The most perceptive witness to this was Ian Sellar. Now an established feature director himself with *Venus Peter* and *Prague*, Sellar, then a student of photography, met Iain Smith in a pub. Smith's own career in film production commenced with *My Childhood* (his mother was acting in the film), though Hassan, entirely at his own behest, was to sack him. This chance encounter led Ian Sellar to enter the scene and, for better or worse, to be put in charge of continuity.

Continuity was not easy. Sellar had to ensure that the whippet, the boys and Douglas were available on cue. The dog and the boys were difficult enough; Douglas, on certain days, simply went walkabout and was impossible to locate. Sellar felt that such was the intensity of Douglas's vision inside his head that he found it difficult to communicate what he wanted, or that what he wanted would appear irritatingly trivial, even whimsical. For example, Douglas demanded swing-doors for inside the orphanage which no one else could see the need for until they saw the effect produced in the rushes. Sellar was immediately aware of Douglas's obsessed state, which led him to any lengths to get what he wanted. For Sellar, the utter extremism of Douglas's acts came in a relatively small event when the director prepared the poppies which were to be gathered by Tommy and thrown, withered, out of the cup by Jamie:

> Bill got a lighter and withered these poppies. It was a very shocking sight seeing somebody get flowers and deliberately wither them. I couldn't believe it was that important and just a such a surreal thing to see somebody do. It was a very destructive act and it was central to Bill's need to get everything right in a particular way at whatever cost. It's an intensely difficult thing to do to get things that right. I've subsequently worked with quite a few directors and I've never seen anyone come close to what Bill achieved. Everything in that film is, with very few exceptions, exactly how he wanted it and how he saw it. Due to such precision and clarity in everything being done, it was very exciting to experience because suddenly you saw something fit his vision. Because I was doing continuity I used to look through the camera a lot and suddenly, though you weren't sure what the whole vision was, you would see with amazing precision a world and landscape that was in itself very imprecise.

Despite rumours of an endangered canary, fortunately Douglas's ruthlessness did not extend beyond plant life. The cat was acquired, dead, from Edinburgh. Douglas then decided not to use it, so that it was buried for four days before being retrieved. Other acts of improvisation caused less dismay. Sellar remains astonished by Douglas's cinematic sleights of hand so that apparently totally tangible things could be conjured out of almost nothing. This was especially true with the mine shots. For example, one extraordinary shot of miners underground was actually made at night in Edinburgh with students in a boating pond. Sellar still thinks of doing continuity on the first two films as his hardest job in cinema. He felt, however, that the film crew were welded together into a sort of army, despite the friction, both by Douglas's creative intensity and by Hassan's belief in the importance of Douglas as an artist. Hassan's particular belief in Douglas was strengthened by a spontaneous sympathy for several Scottish directors and a still unrequited desire to see a truly ethnic Scottish cinema. He was, rightly, nicknamed MacMoun by the Scottish members of the crew.

Geoffrey Evans had to leave before completion to take up an acting job, and Brian Crumlish, a Scottish contemporary of Douglas's at the London Film School, took over production. Crumlish is perfectly frank that he deplored Douglas's directorial manner then and has never been convinced of the cinematic style it produced, finding it static and mannered. Their disagreements, however, illuminate the essential narrative mode of what Douglas was trying to achieve. Thus Douglas reported to Hassan: 'At bottom Crumlish disliked my preference for the fixed camera and saw the hand-held camera as a great revolutionary move forward. I will not discuss the zooms I did not want until I see the rushes.' Douglas was obsessed with the notion that film should not provide information but drama; as in life, the audience should be surprised. It was this principle that led to the ultimate confrontation with Crumlish over the film's conclusion.

Crumlish and Douglas give different accounts of what happened; or, it should be said, Crumlish recalled the ending that was not used, Douglas recalled the ending that was. Crumlish's version is that Douglas was enraged with Iain Smith, who had been sent to acquire a steam-making machine for the shot of Jamie jumping off the bridge and returned from Edinburgh with a quite inadequate theatrical smoke-making device. Crumlish and Smith set out for Edinburgh to acquire an appropriate machine. When they returned, they found Douglas and a crestfallen crew having tea. Eventually they learned that a still furious Douglas had filmed the conclusion of the film with Jamie committing suicide by jumping off the bridge into the path of an oncoming train. Crumlish phoned Hassan who, he alleges, was equally furious and demanded a reshoot, not so much to save Jamie's life as to ensure that the other parts of the *Trilogy* would be made. The Douglas version is, presumably, of this later shoot:

> There was no suitable gadget to create the smoke. I also gave Crumlish plenty of notice to contact the Tranent Fire Brigade for a safety blanket. The boy was to fall into the cover and save me killing him! Crumlish returns on the actual day of the filming and tells me that the fire brigade had nothing for safe falls. Well, I thought, if it kills me I'll prove that such a blanket does

exist *and it does*.

Crumlish's easy solution is to tell me to alter the ending as I have an obligation, *as if I didn't know*. So there I am on the bridge – no smoke that will work except for a close-up and no safety blanket for the boy. Crumlish reminds me that it is cruel what I am making the boy do. There lies his reason for not finding the necessary props. He wants to rewrite the scene.

The cry went out, 'Just let the boy run away.' True, a very simple ending. Also very predictable and a bore. I tried very hard while writing that script to keep two things running parallel and opposite in each scene. For instance, there was the possibility of two ideas floating through the audience's mind – suicide or survival. Running was nothing but a yawn.

I have written this letter because I loathe indifference. I am grateful to the BFI for the chance to make *Jamie* and to you for your encouragement but the film is not anywhere near what I wanted and that does not make me a bit happy. Now I want to get out of this country and go home.

MY AIN FOLK

The international success of *My Childhood* did not mean that the making of *My Ain Folk* was less problematic and stressful. In fact, especially in the editing process, things became significantly worse. In part, this was because Douglas was recreating the most painful period of his own childhood. But also this was a formally more complex film in that he was attempting a narrative form which involved the complete synchronisation of the audience's conscious awareness with that of the child. Arguably the biggest pressure on him, however, was that, because of the success at the Venice festival, Douglas was no longer an anonymous grantee of the BFI but at the forefront of the Board's consciousness and ambitions. This did not at all suit him:

What you had on *My Childhood* was a grantee, treated like any other grantee. He filled in his application form and waited while his script took the upward climb to acceptance. The procedure was normal and it suited my nature.

The same was not true of *My Ain Folk*. The exact reverse was the case. The script began its life with the top brass, made its descent and finally took a downward slope into the files. Naturally, their interest pleased me. But it was a bad omen.

There was no such intrusion regarding Douglas's submitted script. Intrusion, partly provoked by Douglas himself, came in the painful, prolonged editing process. As the crew assembled in Newcraighall, the shadows cast by the troublesomely erratic November light indicated both technical problems and Douglas's state of mind. When the BBC wished to include the making of *My Ain Folk* in the *Cinema Now* series, Douglas thought that the director, Trevor Peters, had exceeded his brief both by wasting the crew's time by filming them apparently at work and, worse, by seeking confidential information in the village. His overwrought state of mind regarding personal and project privacy is evident in a letter to Hassan threatening, if Peters used unauthorised material, to sue him for 'making me mentally sick where I want nothing more to do with the film business'. Peters's film, as shown, makes no such transgressions and is most memorable for the pleasure and enthusiasm evident in locals like Elsie Restorick and Jessie Combe regarding their creative participation in the filming.

The first week's filming went disastrously. Douglas's minder, Ian Sellar, found his charge's capacity to disappear even more finely honed. Worse, he discovered that Douglas was attempting to have him sacked for providing wrongly shaped jam-jars. More than anything else, this confirms Hassan's 'sacrificial' thesis, since not only was Douglas not normally a stickler for nostalgia-

Directing *My Ain Folk*

provoking period accuracy but he ever after, rightly, lavished praise on Sellar for his quick, intelligent, responsive work on set. Tony Bicât, the rather sensitive production assistant, cracked up almost immediately, leaving the more pragmatic Nick Nacht to see the film through – not without, later in the shoot, briefly coming to blows with Douglas. Things could not have so continued without a major explosion which, when it came, cast the whole project in doubt. This explosion unfortunately involved the soundman, Peter Harvey, the virtues of whose technical abilities resonate through the film. The scene involved was when the social worker comes to take Tommy away and a ferocious struggle breaks out. Douglas always played these physical struggles to the edge. Helena Gloag had already nearly throttled Jessie Combe in their fight scene. Douglas, consequently, hired an extremely powerful local man to play the part, a man who 'could have broken one of the kid's backs in a single bear hug.' He describes the fight thus:

It was a hair-raising scene. And I was a bag of nerves for the kids' safety. On the first scene everyone was a bit too cautious; the second a little better; but the third was totally frightening. The smaller boy ended up a mess of bloody knees, purple bruises and tears. On approaching him, with the intention of first aid, he swiped out at me in anger. The only way I could cope was to

On the set

sling him over my shoulder fireman-style and race him all thumping and kicking to the nearest sink. The other two lay an exhausted mess on the floor.

Back on set, I listened to the playback. It was electric. The scene was in the can. Or so I thought.

Peter Harvey, to his intense mortification, found he had erased this take. He told Douglas on the way back to the hotel. A devastated Douglas was utterly unable to respond. Later he slipped out of the hotel to re-engage the services of his local muscle-man. After a 'nightmare journey from pub to pub', Douglas found him:

He was with his cronies, all bull-headed and ferociously raw like himself. I set to explain my predicament but it was difficult getting through to him for the drink. Somebody snarled something about having a party, and before I knew it we were carrying out plastic bags of booze, and all out of my pocket. I followed them along roads that never seemed to end till we came to his door. Inside, everybody was celebrating except me. The more drink I put away to please them, the more sick in the stomach I became. I flew to the toilet hoping to stop the fairground in my guts. I was staring into the slime wondering if this is what film-making was all about when he walked in. He piddled in the bowl. 'I'll do it for sixty,' he said. He was trebling his salary. I pleaded that I couldn't afford it. Well, in that case, I'd have to get somebody else, wouldn't I? Of course, he knew I needed him because of his appearance in other scenes. I went up to forty. He came down to fifty. What the hell, I thought, looking around me I could see they were poor, even desperate. And after all, isn't life more important than art?

Still vomiting, Douglas made it back to the hotel, the sleeping crew and the script for the next morning:

I reached for my shooting script, chucked it, couldn't cope. I shut my eyes and saw the fight happening all over again. I leapt up frightened by the strong man going too far. I stood by my typewriter cursing myself for ever having written such a scene, and I was full of bitterness for ever having lived such a scene. Something inside me cracked.

In the morning the typewriter lay a tangled mess on the floor. And an innocent chair ended up as firewood. Where I had not been able to vent my wrath at Harvey, now I ordered him to put my typewriter to rights. Justice was done, or perhaps I should say only half done, for one of the crew cabled London. Mamoun Hassan, then Head of the Production Board, flew up. In fine controlled outrage he told me shooting was over. And paid for the chair. Perhaps he had a word with the cameraman or even Harvey himself, for he just as soon changed his mind.

The conclusion was not quite so clear-cut. Hassan also had to deal with a suicide threat from Douglas, uttered in a telephone box with the cord round his neck. Charles Rees always believed that Hassan had the perceptive strength to deal with any crisis Douglas could throw at him. Hassan, for his part, worked on the assumptions that the power of his art emerged from the turmoil of contradictions within Douglas's Scottish personality and that his strongest single impulse was not self-destruction but the creative making of film.

As the crisis developed, Charles Rees, partly on the strength of owning a Volvo car, had been summoned from London by Hassan to help with production. Rees, a highly skilled editor, had, to his eternal regret, turned down an offer to edit *My Childhood*. Helping in production, he felt amateurishly inadequate. Rees still feels guilty about not being able to supply Douglas in a Scottish November with a dried-out stream for the scene between the grandfather and his fancy woman. Rees feels that the experience was a cross between a polar expedition and by far his most important experience in film. Douglas wanted solidarity but was, in production terms, extremely bad at communicating, and an atmosphere of distrust soon developed. While the more perceptive of the crew realised the fundamental cinematic importance of what they were doing, things were so bad that, when they got off the London train for their first hot bath in weeks, more than half the crew could not bring themselves to say goodbye to Douglas.

The editing of *My Ain Folk* commenced in London at the beginning of 1973. Douglas was working with Brand Thumin, a young, talented but then inexperienced American. Having formed a highly successful partnership, assisted by Hassan's technical expertise, in editing *My Childhood*, they had no obvious reason to think they would not bring it off again. What actually happened was that, six months later, an exhausted Thumin left with no completed or indeed coherent film in sight. Hassan subsequently engaged Peter West, probably then the best young editor at the BBC. West estimated it would take a month of his holidays of full-time work to edit the film. The month was consumed. West started to work with Douglas at weekends, and from 7 p.m. into the small hours. In November, Hassan wrote to Huw Weldon at the BBC seeking West's release for another month. With Douglas, West and Hassan working all through the night on a final cut, the film was rapturously received by a professional audience on 5 December at the London Film Festival.

The bare chronological bones cover a frantic, even farcical year. Towards the end, Douglas wrote bitterly to Hassan (his epistolary commentary on *My Ain Folk* would have filled a medium-sized novel) accusing the BFI of losing faith in his film since 'Had they any imagination they would have seen the film to be right there in the script.' Or, as Peter West records about his uninterrupted last stage of editing: 'The film wanted to be put into the shape it achieved.' The irony is that it was essentially Douglas's loss of faith, expressed in complex, interrelated psychological and aesthetic problems, which mainly caused the chaos. No period in the making of the *Trilogy* is so heavily documented both in the BFI files and Peter West's correspondence. Writing about it, however, incurs the same danger as editing it: you cannot see the wood for the trees. What follows is a necessarily simplified and, regarding Douglas's states of mind, necessarily speculative account.

Thumin had become joint editor of *My Childhood* by accident. He was in the BFI one day when his attention had been caught by screened rushes of the film. A discussion with Hassan ensued, which led to him being hired. Thumin remembers this period of editing as the happiest he had ever known Douglas to be. While, as we have seen, there was a deliberately audience-provoking 'contrapuntal' narrative in the first film, the narrative form of *My Ain Folk* was much more elliptically ambitious. The fundamental principle of its composition was that at no point should the audience know more than the child. The corollary was that Douglas believed that, other than himself, everyone else involved in the picture should contribute to discrete segments but should not have an overall conception of the story since this would lead them to an interpretative, critical state of mind which would inevitably distort the purity and 'openness' of the script. This worked splendidly with the actors. It caused trouble with the crew since Douglas's lack of communication seemed to come mainly from psychological disturbance rather than from undeclared aesthetic principle. It wreaked havoc with the editing process not least because Douglas himself, plagued by severe anxieties, did not, in editing, adhere to the script. In 1973 Douglas wrote this account of what he felt had gone wrong:

> Pressure began as soon as I mentioned bringing back my two editors (Brand Thumin and Tim Lewis). I was told this was out of the question. Two new names were put to me. I rebelled.

Had the two new people mentioned been unable to get a [union] ticket and been badly in need of work, I would have understood perfectly the need to give someone else a chance. But these two were both ticket holders and both inundated with work. The editor, as it turned out, was working two projects at the same time.

But, at first, I rebelled out of a sense of loyalty. Thumin and Lewis started work. Unfortunately the working atmosphere was made deplorable. The two people I had rejected were friends of the Head of the Production Board and I understood that I was going to have to suffer for my preference. Well, it was done. There was no turning back. There was nothing I could do about it. But as always happens to me in a moody atmosphere I found it very difficult to concentrate.

But we came up with the first cut of *My Ain Folk*. This event brought out the top brass, an unusual occurrence since interested parties normally withheld their interest to a later date, to a near fine cut of the finished picture. Diverse criticisms loomed forth and the result was a kind of chaos. I felt more and more the film being taken out of my grasp. The good free days of *My Childhood* were over. Whether I liked it or not I was going to be controlled. I became extremely unhappy. I found myself being squeezed into a mould of expression that was safe but deadly to the way I wanted to do things. Thumin and Lewis were sacked. The two people I had rejected took over.

In fact Douglas, in this first phase of editing, was at least as much agent as victim of what went wrong. As Thumin was well aware, Hassan from the start did not want him as editor. Also, as he and Douglas got bogged down, Hassan became increasingly anxious because of his ambitions for the film and organised frequent screenings to heavyweights in the industry, some of whose suggestions were not helpful. One suggestion, which was to haunt the rest of the editing, was that the film should be broken up in five places with inter-titles to explain to the audience what was happening. This would have been both a confession of narrative failure and wholly against the grain of Douglas's use of the image. Such titles were actually composed but, in the end, fortunately never used.

Another battle that Douglas fortunately won was over the opening Technicolor section from *Lassie Come Home*. Although Michael Relph (then chairman of the BFI Production Board) finally acquired it cheaply, it seemed at first that the cost of the footage from MGM would prove prohibitive. Hassan suggested that Douglas and Thumin view *Bonnie Prince Charlie* in the hope that cheaper, kitsch

landscape material would be forthcoming. Douglas was outraged and, initially, refused to go and view it. All editing ground to a halt. He and Thumin did eventually see the film and found it unusable. Trapped between pressures from above and Douglas's intrusive obsession with minutiae, Thumin felt the whole thing becoming nightmarish. 'Bill,' he records, 'was in a state of depression every other day and, when I say depression, I mean you see a person one day and he is a person and the next day he is sitting, monosyllabic, with his face grey as cement and looks like someone else.'

Directors, as Thumin noted, returning image-saturated from location, are often far too close to what they have just done to have any of the conceptual, functional objectivity needed in editing. Ironically, too, all editors involved with Douglas have stressed that as opposed to the structural precision of his scriptwriting, he had no apparent sense of rhythm in the cutting room. Along with these major problems, Thumin was also aware that Douglas's recreation of the past both fascinated and repelled him, to the severe detriment of the editing process. In writing, as we have seen, Douglas had a trance-like access to his past. In editing, however, this problematic gift became wholly counter-productive so that, in Thumin's words, 'in trying to recapture the essence of the past, he developed an impossible kind of desire to be there, at which point it ceased to be a film and became something else.' As well as this impractical absorption there was a counter-impulse, since Douglas, in recreating the most exposed and painful period of his childhood under Granny Douglas's roof, 'would be deeply shaken by coming into contact with the material to the point he was unable to look at it.' Disastrously, this led Douglas to reject some of the most powerful footage.

With Douglas constantly in such a state and an increasingly fretting Hassan, Thumin's task was impossible. The film's narrative structure and hence its rhythm went badly askew. They achieved a cut of the first reel so fine that, when Thumin ran it, it sped past his astonished eyes like 'an express train'. Douglas also started permutating shots, playing alternative possibilities, and Thumin said he has never seen so many cuts in any film. Clarification would be achieved by Thumin reverting to the original script, where narrative sense, oblique but coherent, would reappear. Thumin realised the compositional principle of the script just before he stopped working on it: 'It was written in a sort of funny kind of way like a detective story where the audience was never meant to discover what was going on ahead of Jamie.' Thumin still believes Douglas was too naive, too intuitive a writer to have so structured things. From what happened next with his second

Previous page: Stephen on the set of *My Ain Folk*

editor, Peter West, Douglas was utterly aware of what he had composed and the continued need to obscure that composition. His mode of recalling what then transpired belongs to the falsely naive. He hid both his profound intelligence and his sophisticated deviousness very well. His memoirs of editing *My Ain Folk* are all, sadly, written in the latter mode.

> I was not allowed to work any more. My new editor would not communicate with me in person. He had not seen *My Childhood* and so, naturally, he did not understand my way of working. He worked the film, as predicted, in that safe but deadly way and there was nothing I could do. I got the message, went home. I communicated with him by letter but got no reply.
>
> Several weeks later I rang and asked if I could come and see what was happening on the picture. He told me if I did he would walk out. Well, the thought of another editor coming in, yet another stranger, was too much. I gave in.
>
> Many weeks later I was invited to a viewing. I noticed my correspondence had not gone unnoticed. The film was going along almost completely shot by shot as scripted by me. When a diversion took place from the original conception, the scene did not work. I made comments but little attention was given to them.

This is such a distortion of what actually went on that Douglas's account of his relationship with Peter West, Hassan and the BFI Production Board over the second half of 1973 is a travesty. West was not, initially, a distant figure. Like Thumin, he made the mistake of letting Douglas work with him in the cutting room. At its worst, this led to Douglas, a parodic Penelope, re-editing by day what West had done in the evening. Far from communicating only by letter, which he did incessantly, Douglas actually lived with West at the latter's expense for a month. Douglas throughout this period was completely obsessed with regaining editorial possession of the film and quite unscrupulous in his methods of so doing. He wrote to Hassan, for example, that West was slow and getting paid for work he, Douglas, was doing. Hassan, enraged, responded that Douglas and Thumin had got nowhere in eight months and that West was getting £100 for expenses. Such a level of provocation could only lead to both sides going over the top. What got West involved, what kept him going, was the poetic intensity of Douglas's footage. As he recorded:

> Bill was not an intellectual but what got me switched on was the intense

quality of poetry which was so unusual and unlike any other British film director (I've known a lot of them) I've ever known. It's impossible to define poetry but if you're any good you recognise it and that's what kept us all going.

West also believes that Douglas could 'articulate perceptions of human conflict like no one else I've ever worked with.' West could justifiably have been ironic here because, as with Thumin, the cutting room became 'a place of glowering tension with a poisonous aura'. West found that a strong element of the problem was the intrusion of the past into the present functional task.

> He became more and more obsessive about certain aspects of the film that were to do with his own inability to dissociate himself from the actual life that he lived and the artefact he created. This caused him to ask for scenes to be cut or dropped. For example the father he had created on screen so disturbed him that he wanted the role diminished. Thus a relatively simple scene with the boy on the road with the father took months to edit.

Things could not go on like this. On 11 August came the notorious incident when Douglas was ejected from the BFI and subsequently threatened with police action. Douglas reported it thus:

> One day, the editor rang me to say a particular scene did not work and would be better out. I pointed out the need to construct in a certain way. He was sceptical. I offered to come and show him what I meant. He agreed.
>
> I arrived at the appointed hour but unfortunately the editor was not available. He was having to meet a deadline on the film he was working simultaneously with mine. No matter. I studied the troubled scene on the editing machine. The telephone rang. Someone answered and handed the phone to me. It was the Head of the Production Board speaking. He was in a fury. He wanted to know why I was in the building. I tried to explain but he heard nothing. He wanted to know why I was working behind the editor's back editing the film. Once more I tried to explain but in his fury he heard nothing. He ordered me out, reminding me I was trespassing on British Film Institute property.
>
> Suddenly I was communicating with him. I said something about not being able to function in this atmosphere. He replied by replacing the receiver. I was feeling pretty shaky, not knowing what to do. I longed to tell

someone, anyone who could help, how hamstrung I was. But I was too frightened to open my mouth. The next thing I knew there was a man in front of me. He was from another part of the building. He told me I was to vacate the premises immediately or he was to ring the police.

I left the building taking a can of film away as a form of protest. Returning home, there was another call telling me the police had been informed that I had stolen BFI property.

I returned the can of film. I stayed at home to accept my position. There was to be no communication between the Board and me whatsoever.

If Douglas was innocent in this particular situation, the general level of his editorial sins was such that Hassan's behaviour on this occasion is quite understandable. Nor, if that was Hassan's intention, did communication terminate. And later in the month Douglas almost got his way. West took ill. There is an unsent draft letter in the BFI files in which Hassan tells Douglas he can, with whatever help he needs, take over editing the film again. Fortunately West recovered and Lindsay Anderson entered the scene. Douglas, in attempting to influence West, had kept alluding to Anderson; West consequently invited Anderson to come along and see how things were going. Anderson was appalled and told Douglas the best thing he could do was leave everything to West and take

Having fun on the set of *My Ain Folk*

four weeks' holiday. Douglas apparently surrendered, allowing a situation which would 'leave you and Anderson with maximum freedom'. Douglas departed for three weeks' holiday, but wrote to Hassan:

> I am, however, a bit disturbed about one thing before I go. It will save time if I say it now and not later. Now, Peter informed me on the phone that he had the continuity sheets at home with him. I think this is dangerous. It will encourage him to think too much which is the worst thing he could do as regards this film. If he weaves the film back and forth in his mind he will be setting himself up as a critic and as a result (undoubtedly) he will start rewriting. He will be saying to himself, 'Oh, we can't leave him doing that here, because there he contradicts himself', to mention one kind of thinking.
>
> I really think it would help him more if he worked in a forward manner, isolating each scene and working it for what it has to offer. He should not concern himself with what happens up the script, and as will happen when he progresses further, what happens or happened down the script. If he doesn't do this and is confused he will not be happy working certain sections of the film.
>
> ... I really think it would be a help to Peter now if he broke the film into scenes, took them out of the continuity of the film, stuck back leader front and end, worked that, put it aside and onto another and so on until he got through the film. It might also help him in this respect if he worked them out of continuity like pieces of a jigsaw.
>
> Of course, what Peter has to decide is where a scene begins and where it ends. There are some short and some very long. As you know the beginning of the film through the cry of 'Tommy' across the landscape is one long continuous scene. And that is how he has worked it in reel 1 and it was very good. The next scene begins at the bathing and ... where it ends is a problem and the subject of the next paragraph.

There then followed five pages of both detailed analysis and actual rewriting of the script. Douglas was asking the utterly impossible of any editor. What saved the day was that West after these many weeks did acquire from Hassan the original script which Douglas had done everything to keep from him. Everything fell into place. West found that Douglas had not only deviated from the script but had abandoned some of the original footage because he thought it did not work. When this was reinserted, the film made the sense it had when written. It would be pleasant to report that this was the happy end of the matter. Douglas went to

Tehran at the beginning of November to receive a prize of *My Childhood*. He returned, and though complaining bitterly to Michael Relph about his lack of fiscal reward for all his work, offered to use his prize money to bring the dub up to what he felt was a proper standard. The film was shown at the beginning of December. In early January 1974, Douglas was still pressing for changes. West said that if these changes to the original script were made he would ask for his name to be removed from the credits. Michael Relph and Keith Lucas (then Director of the BFI) blew the whistle. Douglas and West remained friends throughout Douglas's life. West had agreed with Hassan to edit *Confessions*, presumably, like Thumin, if Douglas were allowed nowhere near the cutting room. He also thinks that these few months had a radical influence in his growth from editor to documentary director.

MY WAY HOME

If the ending of *My Ain Folk* saw relationships between Douglas and the BFI at a low ebb, *My Way Home* also began in less than propitious fashion. Because Stephen Archibald had to grow physically into the part, there had been a three-year cooling off period. Trouble, this time not of Douglas's making, broke out immediately over the script. Mamoun Hassan was in the process of leaving the BFI to take over the National Film Finance Corporation (NFFC). Charles Rees was temporarily holding the production fort before Barrie Gavin and later Peter Sainsbury took over. Douglas submitted the script and seems to have asked Charles Rees to send it to Mamoun Hassan, then in Syria. Hassan, unwisely, replied that, if Douglas had so requested, Rees should quote relevant passages of his reactions. Rees complied, and Douglas was devastated: his relationship with Mamoun Hassan, important to both of them, never fully recovered from Hassan's missive. Hassan began by saying he believed the script was vintage Douglas: 'Yes, enough of that old hate to see him through yet another near masterpiece.' His subsequent diagnosis, however, was that the script oscillated between Douglas at his best and someone who was no longer seeing with individual visionary intensity and trying to compensate with 'fine' writing and external cinematic influences. He wrote:

> [*My Childhood* and *My Ain Folk*] are characterised by an unbearable intensity of vision. The films were made to set the record straight. They were also acts of revenge redeemed by the fact that he did create real characters – in

itself an act of creation; an act of love, if you like. Also they were unconscious acts. Bill was more concerned with what he was seeing than with how he was seen. The new script is nothing like that. *My Way Home* is an explanation and an apology. The vision is no longer intense so he tries to intensify the image. Hence all this over-writing. He is now no longer an original film-maker but trying to be one with borrowings from the New Wave and, heaven help us, from one Bill Douglas.

You may think that a bit unjust, but gone for me that epic simplicity – This is How It Was and Is – to be replaced by Explanations. This is what my dad, my granny and the world did to me, and that is why I am what I am. Of course, such material has been the basis of great art, but in Bill's case it transforms the script into a private diary – something that he successfully avoided in the past. I sympathise with Bill's predicament as a human being, but I don't necessarily want to see it on the screen.

Compare Patrick in *My Way Home* with almost any character from *My Childhood* and *My Ain Folk*. Patrick is intelligent, nice, generous and totally without life. He is there simply to explain how Bill got to here and now. Which brings me to the narrative and the structure.

I think that *My Way Home* ought to be subtitled 'Parts three and fourteen'. I think the flashforward in time is completely unconvincing. So are the flashbacks. For God's sake, how can you have flashbacks in a trilogy? For a moment I thought we were going to have long excerpts from *My Childhood* and *My Ain Folk*. But again they are simply there to explain.

Bill is not a clever film-maker, he is an inspired one. I don't believe that he can *see* half this script and he will flounder. He will not be able to get himself out of trouble during these moments when he is not at one with the material. It'll be a disaster.

The generous thing would be to turn it down.

To be fair to Hassan, the draft he read was not the final one. 'Patrick' not only became 'Robert' but also a wholly credible character. It is hard to believe, however, that the edgy, homoerotic ambivalence that Hassan had so admired in *Come Dancing* (and which was to be at the core of Douglas's adaptation of the *Confessions*, which he requested Douglas to write and was, and still is, keen to produce) was entirely lacking from the first draft. Hassan is a proponent of ethnic cinema, and his sense of Douglas was also fundamentally conditioned by Douglas's Scottishness. He still believes that Douglas, as a Scottish film-maker, was subject to a geographical boundary to his talent which made him incapable of filming *creatively* outside Scotland. Thus of the unmade scripts Hassan thinks everything of *Confessions* and little of Douglas's American script, *Flying Horse*. That Douglas's Scottish creativity was energised by the agonies of personal fission and 'that old hate' was for Hassan the acceptable price of its artistic achievement. Arguably Hassan's judgment of Douglas as man and artist is, for all its keenness, subject to arrested development. Ironically, had Hassan stayed at the BFI, the third part might never have been made.

Douglas was so devastated by Hassan's letter because his own conception of *My Way Home* was that it was an evolution in his film-making: 'I have tried to adapt the style to the situation, incorporating elements from *My Childhood* and *My Ain Folk* to reach for a freer and more diverse expression. *My Way Home* is a journey of self-discovery and the imagery attempts to reflect this.' Fortunately, help was at hand. Hassan had asked Rees to copy his letter to Michael Relph and Stanley Reed. This elicited from Reed the kind of letter that authors dream of receiving about their work. In eleven detailed pages, Reed demonstrated not only a complete grasp of the structural, visual elements of the script but a sympathetic affinity with the precise details of the key problem which is the saving relationship between Robert and Jamie. 'The problem,' Reed wrote, 'is the more difficult in that the *deus ex machina* who effects Jamie's escape is of all things a public schoolboy and his method patronage, out of wealth. He can so easily become a sort of Mr Brownlow to Jamie's Oliver. Middle-class Dickensian do-gooders are not much in favour.'

Unfortunately Stanley Reed had now retired and his creative empathy with Douglas's work was the exception to the rule of the post-Hassan BFI Production Board. Under Peter Sainsbury, what came into vogue at the Production Board was an allegedly innovative cinematic formalism and a Marxist ideology. *My Way Home* was grudgingly accepted, not because the new regime believed in it, but because the dynamic of critical and relative financial success of the first two parts made it difficult to reject. To understand this, we have to see that Douglas was, quite unintentionally, a key element in the struggle that went on within the BFI for some years before Sainsbury reversed Hassan's policy of attempting to make feature films which could be 'commercially' distributed. The lines of this struggle can be discerned in Trevor Peters's 1972 *Cinema Now* documentary. After a comment about Douglas needing BFI money and the BFI needing the publicity of his films – not the best grounds for living together – an argument develops about whether Douglas should now be directed towards the mainstream film industry and TV. Malcolm Le Grice's assertion that this should be so was immediately countered by David Storey, a great enthusiast for Douglas's work:

The boy's only made one 50-minute film. To try and make him into a kind of film hustler, or for us to hustle on his own behalf, I think it really is premature, and again I think it's a very destructive policy – with this particular kind of film, which is very sensitive and very difficult to make in fact, under any circumstances, let alone this one.

Storey's viewpoint, at that time, won an easy majority. Le Grice's opposing view delineates, however, the alternative position regarding radical formal cinema which was to develop later in the decade a more radical political ideology:

Well, there's a whole area of independent film production – one is in political directions and the other is avant-garde experimental in the formal sense. Now the Production Board has never at any point in its history been able to deal with this significant aspect of cinema. It's concentrated on a kind of fringe of the film industry, its terms of references and methods of production have been largely the same as those in the industry, and it's never found a way of dealing with what seems to me the most significant aspect of new approaches to cinema.

If by 1972 Douglas's work could be seen by cinematic radicals within the BFI as formally conservative, *My Way Home*, where the working-class hero's salvation is by means of upper-class intervention towards personal 'high' cultural growth, must have seemed anathema to them. Scottish theoretical Marxists of that period possibly had the added outrage of Robert being English. In any case their antipathy to Douglas, the alleged 'realist', was such that in a volume on Scottish cinema, *Scotch Reels*, Douglas's work went completely unmentioned. Among its manifold political virtues, *My Way Home* is incomparably the finest cinematic account of the collusion of 'tartanry', social class and imperialism. Douglas, in fact, met none of the theoretical prescriptions of such politically radical film aesthetics, whose proponents found him either a dull realist or an excrescent poet who properly belonged to the commercial world which they despised. They saw nothing in his work of the sort of formal innovation which, they believed, was the aesthetic microcosm out of which the future new political macrocosm would emerge. This would be a non-hierarchical democracy. Thus the new cinema would, as prescient of the future, emerge out of non-individualistic, leaderless, indeed prelapsarian groups devoid of envy or ego. Douglas, then, represented for them a decadent bourgeois 'artist' whose films were barely covert forms of the prevailing commercial sickness.

While it would require an extended study to explicate the full, contentious complexity of the quarrel between Sainsbury's new policy and that prevailing under Hassan, some indication of its depth and extent is needed in order to understand fully the problems of *My Way Home*. This quarrel reached a climax just prior to the making of the last part of the *Trilogy* with the publication of Alan Lovell's programme for a season of Production Board Films, including Douglas's, which asserted that 'the overall impact of the films produced is somewhat dispiriting ... The general level of achievement seems low.' Even more remarkably, Lovell noted that 'effectively the Fund/Board has operated to confirm the status quo in independent film-making.' This led to Hassan (with others such as Lindsay Anderson, Kevin Brownlow, Margaret Matheson and Philip French) publishing an opposing broadsheet which, among other things, pointed out that Lovell (who was in the BFI Education department) had always opposed Board policy and was the last person to write such a programme. It concluded:

> In our view this season is not a celebration of what is most dynamic and challenging in independent cinema but an attempt at manipulation of the film-makers' works in pursuit of petty political purposes within the BFI. ('British Film Institute Production Board: a broadsheet from former board members and grantees', published in *Rough Cut*, Special Issue, 1976)

Lovell seems to have been invited to write his denigratory history of significant achievement in order to allow Sainsbury more freedom to change production policy. Hassan, in a subsequent interview, pointed out that the Production Board was imperilling artistic freedom with its obsession with an ideological purity of motive which it seemed to find only among group film-makers. Hassan was incensed that the films his regime had sponsored were seen not only as formally conventional but politically collusive with establishment values. His analysis of how Douglas was perceived within the BFI anticipates the trouble that followed:

> Well, you have to accept that at the BFI there are a lot of people who think that the films should not be made, that they are kind of – how was it described to me by Barrie Gavin? – necrophiliac acts. What they think necessary is to go into group film-making and documentaries. They don't like Bill Douglas's movies, or at least only in as much as they relate to the working class, which Bill is not interested with at all. The BFI has become entirely concerned with motive and not with the life of films. ('Concrete Policies for Concrete Minds', in *Rough Cut*, Special Issue, 1976)

To tease out all the implications of this value system lies outside the present study. What can be said is that as a concept of the actual sociological state of British cinema it was bizarre, and, with particular regard to the making of *My Way Home* and the subsequent 'distribution' of the *Trilogy*, it led to behaviour both ludicrous and destructive.

The basic problem in distributing the *Trilogy*, and comparable British films of creative merit, was not so much the location of an audience but the lack of an infrastructure of cinemas in Britain willing to show such films. Had the great enthusiasm of George Hoellering and his Academy Cinema for Douglas's work been replicated throughout the major British cities, the problem might have been solved. Douglas's own qualified hope was that this sort of work would create a new audience. His sadness was that the people about whom the films were made were almost wholly resistant to them:

> I was hoping it would go to people who somehow could relate to that kind of environment. I tried to get at people near the ground and living ordinary lives, which I don't think you see – I'm not saying I got it – but I don't think you see so much in the commercial cinema. And I was hoping these people would come, but now I know it's students ...

Le Grice and subsequent like-minded associates on the Production Board committee operated on the tacit, illogical assumption that their new more demanding, or confusing, formalism was the political tool to enlighten the masses. In the 1972 *Cinema Now* programme Michael Relph forcefully pointed out that such a policy would lead to an audience confined to the film-makers themselves:

> One of the criteria that we apply is that they must communicate in some way. They must not be so far out that they communicate with nobody. But it must be a communication with a minority. But we do think that we are helping, even through the limited distribution that our films get, to create a new audience which will ultimately be to the benefit of distributors and exhibitors in the industry as well.

Both Douglas and the BFI Production Board at that time anticipated that a more intelligent audience was developing which, in Douglas's words, 'would meet the new cinema if they got a chance to meet it.' By 1978 the notion that Douglas was a seminal figure in bridging the gulf between British 'art' and commercial cinema was the antithesis of Production Board policy. Hence we find Peter Sainsbury, in addressing the problem of production policy, saying:

> While the BFI has always distanced its production funding from the
> obviously commercial and given support to projects motivated by intentions
> other than the entrepreneurial it has, over the past four years, quite con-
> spicuously pursued a policy resulting in even less marketable films. It has
> done so for good reason. The generation of film-makers applying to the
> Board for production funds in this recent period have been frequently
> concerned with nothing less than a reinvention of the communication pro-
> cess itself, with the idea that the so-called 'language of cinema' is not limited
> to the familiar lexicon and syntax of naturalist and realist forms; that it
> must be freed from such forms if it is to express ideas about the world other
> than those expressed through the industrialised modes of production – both
> cinema and television – and that alternative methods of distribution need to
> be developed toward a more productive relationship between film-maker
> and audience. ('Production Policy', in *The New Social Function of Cinema,
> BFI Production Catalogue 79/80*, pp. 8–9)

If such 'alternative methods' resulting from 'strategic thinking as opposed to
radical postures' could be devised, Douglas was certainly not to be a beneficiary.
Credited with bringing 'an almost Bressonian poetic into the tradition of British
realism', he was damned by working with the conventions of 'familiar cinema
traditions'. He was certainly not to be of the radical elect. Witness this tortuous
definition of the Production Board's role:

> The original definition of the Board's activity – the funding of small appren-
> tice works – remains a proper definition in the view of many and combines
> with the guilt that comes from having to reject so many projects each year,
> for lack of money, into a strong resistance to the provision of continuing
> support – even across only two productions – for a given film-maker. The
> result can often be a lost investment. Film-makers disappear into the void
> almost irrespective of the success of their work and one of the ways of
> building an audience for independent cinema – through a continuing public
> interest in a particular kind of work – is cut off. It is unlikely that the vicious
> circle beginning to undermine the credibility of independent cinema, by
> relating lack of audience to lack of resources, will be broken through if the
> Production Board keeps casting about for 'winners' among near beginners.
> The work needs nurturing. (Ibid., p. 11)

If Douglas was to disappear into the void it was not for the lack of as hard a shove as Sainsbury and his cohorts could give. The ironies of this statement speak for themselves. They had, in the making and editing of *My Way Home*, dire practical consequences. Douglas, in the frantic period of editing *My Ain Folk*, had denounced Hassan as behaving like Louis B. Mayer. An outrageous accusation in itself; but Hassan's alleged old-style management paled into insignificance in the face of the new. Douglas's notes include this extract from a visit to John Kobal's, written at the nadir of the making of *My Way Home*:

> Went to Kobal's. He has a sense of humour about life. He can hear me out and roar. Not that he is without understanding. Far from it. So his place is a welcome relief. 'Here he is,' he exclaims. 'The boy from the working class. The boy who really knows what it is to be hungry. And what happens? He finds himself working for the Marxists (Sainsbury & Co.) and they treat him like shit. They get their big wages and their expense accounts and they fuck around. THEY are the real capitalists.' His performance is full of irony and I fall about.

It was against this institutional background that shooting of *My Way Home* began in early October 1978. Richard Craven, an enthusiast for Douglas's earlier films, was in charge of production. He recalls that, before commencing this job, he had been a guest at a party hosted by Charles Rees and Ian Sellar specifically held to inform him of the thorny path that lay ahead. Thorny it certainly was: Craven called a halt after the shooting of the Scottish section of *My Way Home*. Trouble developed almost immediately. Two young, inexperienced assistants were sacked because of confusion about the shooting of apple trees in Kent for the film's last shot. Their response to their removal contains, given precedent, a highly credible analysis of the initial stages of Douglas's filming of the *Trilogy*:

> The real point is that while we fluffed certain things badly, in view of the state of the production as a whole, where the producer is forced to spend his time attending to the emotional needs of the director (as Richard himself puts it), where organisation is the lowest priority, where accusations of conspiracy and opposition produce an atmosphere in which no one but the director makes a decision, but where he never does, these mistakes are inevitable. It is unnecessary to go into detail, but no one's record on this production is clean. No one can stay immune. In our case, if the producer is prevented from doing his job, if production assistants with insufficient

experience, and given no authority, have to second-guess him and the director, mistakes arising from such a situation do not represent sufficient grounds of summary dismissal.

Richard Craven certainly had his hands full. On the one hand, he had what he considered Douglas's almost uncanny ability to position the camera and, on the other, constant turmoil created by Douglas's dissatisfactions with the circumstances of and personnel involved in the shoot. The art director seemed a particular cause of discontent and led to Douglas throwing a chest of drawers down the stairwell of their Edinburgh hotel in the middle of the night. Expulsion was summary and legal action threatened. What broke Craven, however, was that Douglas, despite the agreed shooting schedule, stopped filming instead of continuing with the Egyptian sequence. Whether Douglas had secretly so intended is unknown. His reason for doing so, however, was artistically correct: he believed that Stephen Archibald was simply not big enough to be credible for the role of a National Serviceman. Even with the delay that ensued, Archibald, who had grown up a bit, was still on the small side. In early January 1975 Craven wrote Douglas a letter, copied to the Production Board, the tone of which suggests more sorrow than anger:

> I am surprised as much as grieved that you could let our relationship come to this, a partnership which from the beginning promised a unique cooperation. It is rare that two minds can fuse together in this way and I felt more than ever that I would respect and continue that relationship with special consideration because of the mutual advantages which would inevitably come out of it for both of us. I am very sad that we might not work on future projects together, but your behaviour over the past few weeks has led me to accept that you neither have respect for our relationship, nor indeed any for the people who have helped make your film possible. By continuing as your producer I would be leading you further into a false position where you might believe that such behaviour was acceptable, where more and more you would call upon me to provide that cushioning effect, protecting you from the realities of the actual situations that arise and continually making excuses for your behaviour of which you will not accept responsibility. The threatened legal action of Mrs Muldoon and the subsequent settlement is only one example that people outside will accept such behaviour even less, and it is such people that you will have to rely upon in the business of making films. Ever since you decided to stop filming in the

middle of the schedule that you yourself had approved before filming I have been loyal to you. But such loyalty I now see has led you to believe that you can use me and my persuasiveness to get whatever you want, that a director can stop filming when he wants to, and can discard his responsibilities to the production when he feels like it. It is just as well to learn now that I will not accept such behaviour, nor do I wish to promote it, nor do I care to be associated with it, for it has a diminishing effect on the efforts of everyone who tries to help you.

Given the Scottish events, it might have seemed a trifle optimistic of Douglas to seek ease and redemption under the Egyptian sun. Douglas at his most depressed would not, however, have devised a scenario for what transpired. As therapy after the event, Douglas wrote a longish piece of prose, 'Flight into Egypt'; that this is not a paranoid's diary is supported by Judy Cottam's report and the testimony of other participants in the chaos.

Peter Sainsbury, on other business, had preceded them to Egypt. Strapped for cash and on a tight schedule (a fortnight for preparation and a fortnight for shooting), he was supposed to make initial, facilitating contact with the embassy and the Egyptian military authorities. The film team arrived in the middle of the night to find he had not even booked them into the Lotus Hotel. The soundman's equipment, the RAF uniforms and the film stock all went adrift on the flight. The film was not retrieved until a week before they were due to go home. To the Egyptians, the mere sight of a 35mm camera meant not only Hollywood but the mighty dollar. They had no conception of this British shoestring operation, whose tiny budget was seriously undermined by the £10 per consultation the Hilton doctor charged them for the constant gastric problems which almost all of them had. Douglas, by sheer force of will and liberal doses of alcohol, only surrendered to the 'runs' at the very end of shooting. To the normal labyrinthine levels of Egyptian bureaucracy was added, in the wake of the humiliating defeat by Israel, a war psychosis. As Douglas noted:

> For everywhere and everything a permit was in demand. . . . We learned that it was not uncommon for disheartened film crews to depart back to Austria or Mexico without a single frame of film in the can. . . . The answer was always the same. 'We are in a state of war.' And that, politely, was that.

Douglas, as always, was preoccupied with filming exactly where the actual events had taken place. Indeed, he had with him the very photographs Peter Jewell had

With Satyajit Ray at the Calcutta Film Festival, 1975

pinned to his locker over twenty years before. He had anticipated that he would be able to film at their camp, Abu Sueir, with the physical intimacy of place that had been the case in Newcraighall.

> I knew my locations like the back of my hand. I had only to enter the camp at Abu Sueir to find immediately what I was looking for, and I needed very little: just a billet, a cinema, a bit of barbed wire and a way out of the camp.
>
> The trouble was nobody believed me. I was held at bay as if I was a spy. 'It isn't that we don't trust you. But we are in a state of war.' I pointed out how close I shoot, how static my camera would be, and if it did move – which would be twice – I had no intention of filming their equipment. When I didn't get very far on that one, I made the offer to process the footage right there and let them select what I could and could not have. When even this didn't work, I suggested they provide me with someone to look through the camera and approve for the entire duration of the shoot. I felt a softening up. And so the visit to the Canal Zone was arranged.

When they got there, however, they were not allowed inside the camp because Abu Sueir had become the chief rocket base of the Egyptian army. Scottish resistance to Douglas's will had been as nothing compared to this. In Scotland, at whatever cost, he had almost always got his way; here, the hitherto irresistible force met a series of immovable objects. Compromise in filming was not of his nature, but he had no option. With enormous trouble and delay, alternative locations were set up nearer Cairo. The interior was created in the corner of a police barracks where they had a two-hour period each day when the men were not noisily present. The exterior, costing an extra £100, was a two-wall plywood mock-up which Douglas felt was akin to the sort of structure that would fall around Buster Keaton's ears. To this was added the anxiety of raising the Union Jack over this rickety structure; someone always had to be on hand to haul it down on the approach of Egyptian military aircraft, which might have assumed a post-Suez invasion. Douglas became increasingly irritable and stressed: 'The interrogators filled my dreams and the mosquitoes my bed.' He began to think they might be bugged. Time leaked away and the shooting period became ever more compressed. The actors were due. They did not appear on the day allocated. The BFI remained mainly silently unhelpful throughout. When the telexed news came, it was unbelievably bad. Stephen Archibald's wife Maggie had miscarried; there was some doubt whether Archibald could come. However, David Mingay, the first editor of *My Way Home*, went up to Craigmillar to collect him and put him on the plane. Not so much artistically as personally, this was the last news Douglas wanted to hear:

> I was numbstruck and outraged and hurt. I felt Stephen and Maggie had been betrayed. And all for a film. I had known Maggie was pregnant but kept it to myself for it was something private to them. And they needed protection for it seemed to me nobody at their respective homes was giving it. Underlying this was the loyalty I owed to Stephen.
>
> Hadn't I taken him from the street and stuck him in front of the camera? Hadn't I asked him to stay by me from one film to another in order to see the whole thing through? Whether I liked it or not, I had a responsibility to him. I couldn't play with his life. I had to be aware of the effect, once it was no longer a novelty, this experience would have on him. Of course the inevitable had happened and he wanted to act for the rest of his days.
>
> Stephen and I had been together through thick and thin for seven years. In the films he was me and in reality I identified myself with him. Our relationship had firmly cemented itself. In order to protect him I was careful never to let his private life be invaded. There was much in his life to make a publicist's dream come true. I was frightened of that and determined to keep him whole. If anyone provided a photograph of Stephen, I provided it. And if anyone wanted to speak to him, I spoke, so on top of the human tragedy, I took exception to this telex with its sudden exposure.

Under this pressure Douglas started to berate and drive the crew. Giving Stephen Archibald and Jo Blatchley time to adjust, he set out to film a scene in a village square which, alluding to a nativity tableau, required a mother, a child, a donkey and quietness. Douglas's intention to achieve the last quality in the early morning did not succeed. The sun stood higher in the sky, suitable shadows became increasingly unavailable, a noisy crowd of children gathered and chanted 'Charlton Heston' because the great man had recently filmed in this selfsame square. Mick Audsley, with relatively primitive sound equipment, was driven beyond distraction trying to achieve the perfect synchronisation that Douglas required between sound and frame. From scenes such as these came this glory of the Scottish cinema:

> Eight o'clock became nine became ten. Now the square was full of activity. I determined to make constructive use of the time. I spied a donkey, decided it

would look good in the shed beside the mother and child, and hired it. I needed an Arab boy for a later scene, picked one out and negotiated with his father. Finally came word that the camera was fine.

The woman, the mother of the scene, looked splendid. All humble with lowered eyes. The casting was uncanny in its accuracy. It was yet another example of others knowing instinctively what I was after. It had happened to me so many times before. All I had to do was describe, and either he or she knew. And I went along with them because of some inner conviction that never seemed to fail me. The children started to crowd in on the camera, almost pushing Ray over. The cane flew. I pleaded. And Judy dropped a bomb. They scattered across the square and back again. I pushed up our friend's fee to make them disappear but he couldn't perform that feat at any price.

Then our real trouble came from an adult onlooker, a man. 'This is a disgrace', he shouted from the crowd. 'This scene is an insult to Egypt.' He pointed inside the shed. The woman was sitting on a stool with the child on her lap while nearby stood the donkey. It was true the shed was more suitable for pigs but right I thought to convey the nativity feeling I was trying for. 'They want to take their film outside and tell people this is the real Egypt,' he said. I tried to reason with him. 'This woman is dirty and sitting in a filthy place,' he yelled. He was beside himself. Suddenly, he flew forward to grab at the camera. Hag bear-hugged the man in an effort to pull him back. He said something in Arabic and now the two of them were going strong. I said something about not wanting to hurt anybody. Judy screamed something about Allah and poverty. The man hurried off threatening to fetch the police. I shouted to Ray to shoot the scene quick. You couldn't see us get back to Cairo for dust.

The appearance of the two actors caused contradictory responses. Of Stephen Archibald, Douglas wrote:

If there was hurt going on inside him, he kept it from us. Instead he gave us the best of him, very calm, very understanding, very giving, and with an unexpected sense of humour that made everyone else around look positively drab. I marvelled at him, at the man growing inside him. Gone was the selfish, self-pitying, rebellious, cantankerous though often endearing boy, and I found myself drawn to him anew in sheer respect.

As if to justify Douglas's predilection for the amateur over the professional, Blatchley, however, seemed to him to have metamorphosed from what he had thought in London as ideal casting into a nervy performer lacking in trust in his director. It was an increasing clash of personalites which, as always, expressed itself at first in apparent minutiae. Blatchley developed, as he always did in a new role, a water blister at his mouth; Douglas hated using make-up for his actors. Blatchley refused to trim his eyebrows to make himself look younger. The film's editor, Mick Audsley, recalls Douglas having constantly to wind down Blatchley's performance. When they saw the rushes they realised the degree to which Blatchley had been blinking. Douglas was enraged, making no allowance for hot wind and sand, so they edited out the blinks by taking out two frames. 'Ironically, both Stephen and Jo were exact opposites of what I wanted their characters to be. I could see I was going to have to work overtime to perform miracles on celluloid.'

Douglas's version of overtime caused a near mutiny, with the crew threatening to take the next plane home. As in Newcraighall, Douglas seemed quite incapable of seeing that his phlegmatically English crew were giving their ill-paid all. Judy Cottam much more accurately records the circumstances:

> I cannot say enough about how hard and well everybody worked in very exacting and difficult circumstances. From the arrival of crew and actors, our hours were 5 a.m. till late evening. Everyone mucked in and helped all round, painting props, Ray drawing the billet which was built in the sand, Jo doing costumes. Continuity sheets which I was responsible for got sadly neglected as I often had to leave shooting to look after other problems. Bill and I were very pushed to get everything done as neither of us had assistants; we would no doubt have been a lot more efficient with more help.

Mick Audsley was present as sound recordist not only because he knew Peter West and Peter Harvey – so he knew how difficult it was going to be – but because he had been shaken to the core by the intensity of the first films. Like Ian Sellar, he was astonished by the transformative power of Douglas's shooting.

> I saw these things being shot and you never felt it had happened; there was no evidence of the intensity that appeared subsequently on the screen. You had to be exactly on the axis of the camera to see it. If you were three feet to the left you did not have any sense of a performance having happened at all. For example, in that wonderful kipper scene none of us knew it was in the bag till we saw the rushes. There was this incredibly intense, poetic quality I

have never seen in anybody else's work since. Nor did I even know if Bill knew he had got the shot. You could only watch the performance on film, hence the uniqueness of cinematic experience. Bill was, in a painterly sense, a great primitive. I also remember that when the camera moved for the first time my hair stood on end; Jamie walks toward Robert and the camera goes with him. Bill had never moved the camera before, and when he did it meant something that was quite extraordinary.

If Audsley tended to keep his thoughts to himself, the same cannot be said of Judy Cottam. Douglas rightly noted that 'the resulting film owed everything to her', and his Egyptian memoir is dotted with laughing and ironic comments on Cottam's explosive powers. For example, it was Cottam who eventually did retrieve the mislaid film stock, hitting Cairo airport with more force, Douglas recalled, than the Israelis:

> It was 3 a.m. In her fury she decided not to ring him. She would get him out of bed. The Petts Wood of Cairo was rudely awakened by an incessant ringing of the door bell. Fortunately for the gentleman concerned he was a gentleman. Of course, he understood perfectly. Would she care for a cup of tea? A sherry perhaps? 'No, thank you. All I want is the fucking film. Now.' No doubt he was given a lecture on the Rights of Women for it was her habit to educate wherever she found a need. And she charmed him because this was at the heart of her complex nature. One simple phone call and Judy got her film.

Her charm certainly appealed to Douglas's complex nature; theirs was an intimate friendship which lasted, not without turbulence, till his death. As well as emotional sustenance from Cottam and Archibald, Douglas found some of his Egyptian helpers extraordinary. After Cottam had demonstrated to them the financial sparsity of the operation, Hag, the driver, and Black Abdul, in his sixties yet so strong he could run up dunes with the camera under his arm, behaved with consummate sympathy.

Against all odds the necessary footage was non-sequentially shot. They rushed to the airport. Audsley recalls that Peter West's wife subsequently told him she had to stand back from him on his reappearance because he smelled so bad. There was to be no respite; a crisis quite overshadowing all the Egyptian events blew up. From the Production Board files we find this letter to Douglas's friend, film critic David Robinson, who was apparently en route to Egypt and had offered help with this new, perhaps terminal problem:

> As background information I should tell you that the results of the mechanical fault was 'camera unsteadiness' diagnosed by the lab which printed the material, by the BFI technical officer and by the cameraman sent out by the BFI. This means that the camera pull down mechanism was out of sync with the shutter movement resulting in imperfect registration of the frame. It is rare (as you might know) but hard to surmount. All other causes have been eliminated.

The next day, 18 August, Peter Sainsbury reported to Michael Relph that there were two possible solutions to the problem. One, technically doubtful, was to reshoot the material frame by frame on an Oxberry camera; the other, to shoot from scratch.

> The financial implications are as follows: we have a pre-purchase contract with German Television worth £7,000 and I am attempting to argue within the Institute that we should put this revenue into the production budget; this

With some locals on the Egyptian shoot of *My Way Home*

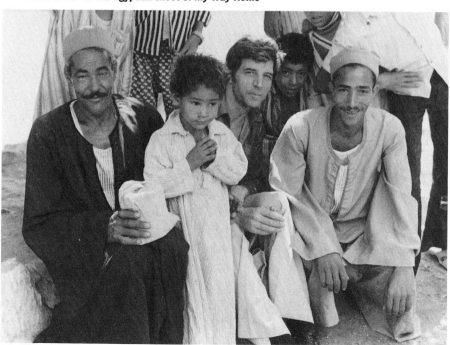

is an unprecedented step and I may well require your support in arguing for this. Bill Douglas and the editors have agreed to produce a version of the film for the Germans to meet their transmission date of the 24th October to ensure that this venue will be forthcoming. The Germans have run a tele-cine test on the material and will accept it in spite of the fact that they agreed with us that it could not possibly be used for cinema projection. This will ensure that we do not overspend what the Production Board has actually allocated to the production.

We failed to detect this fault largely because, shooting on a shoestring as usual, we had neither the time nor the money to process rushes in London during shooting in Cairo. We will therefore have to find further money to correct the problems. Bill is, of course, anxious to reshoot and for this we would require a further £8,000 to £10,000. There is a 50/50 chance that this amount will come from the insurance policy that Nita arranged to cover eventualities of this kind. We have people in Cairo attempting to obtain a supportive statement from the studio where the camera was hired and Lloyds may well accept our claim. If they do not, I will have to ask the Institute (i.e. the Production Board and/or the Executive) to choose between junking the film and coming up with the money. The alternative recourse is to find the money elsewhere and I shall do everything possible to achieve this.

Sainsbury concluded in a rather contradictory manner. His assertion that 'I feel a personal commitment to completing the film to acceptable standard' contrasts with his concluding 'Frankly, I do not expect the Production Board to be sympathetic.' The Board's compassion was never put to the test. It was found that the error lay neither with the camera itself nor with the cameraman Ray Orton, but with faulty processing at the Rank Laboratory. Sainsbury wrote to Orton:

No doubt you are also relieved to have it confirmed that your own work on the film was exemplary. I must say the reprinted material looks very good indeed, and I am sure we will have the best of the Bill Douglas films completed by January.

In fact, the film was not completed until October 1978. What followed was a horrendous series of personal and technical problems, more complex than even the editing of *My Ain Folk*. The first editor of *My Way Home* was David Mingay, a friend of Peter West and another high-quality BBC product. As with all Douglas's editors, Mingay's enthusiasm for the work far exceeded any financial reward. He worked for £50 per week. Douglas, wrongly, never seemed at ease with Mingay in an editorial capacity. He had, however, sufficient caution not to attempt to undermine Mingay as he had nearly succeeded in doing with West. And he kept relatively quiet in the editing room. Mingay found him not infrequently dictatorial, but they worked out a *modus operandi* and under great pressure Mingay put together – by taking certain technical short cuts – a version that could be sold by October 1976 to German TV. Immediately after this Sainsbury retrieved all the material from Mingay's cutting rooms, alleging that there was no more money to polish the final cut.

Mingay was less than pleased, given that he received no extra payment for his pressured work on the German sale, which brought the BFI £7,000 and which, he thought, all went into paying for production so that Douglas also got nothing. What Mingay did not know was that Douglas was, covertly, still obsessed with getting editorial control over his own films. For different reasons Douglas and Sainsbury colluded in dropping Mingay. Thus Douglas to Sainsbury:

> I am not satisfied with David's work. I think maybe it would be better to let him go. But the problem is to find the right person to put the film right. I think Mick (Audsley) will help me to put the first reel into synch.
>
> The right person I was referring to above will be needed to replace the 'Redeemer' and, at Fettes, the missing football sequence (both are lying around from previous goes with Tony and need cutting in).
>
> The op sound track is poor and particularly throughout Egypt and needs sharpening. There are background sounds I can't hear at all and, worse, some dialogue I couldn't hear at all, as in the whole of the first track in Egypt. I don't know if Rank can improve on this or not. But I hope so after all the improvements we've made.

Almost certainly Douglas's intention was that he and Audsley would extend their remit beyond the first reel. That this did not lead to the disastrous, never-ending permutations of *My Ain Folk* stemmed from the fact that Douglas did stick to his own script and to what he and Mingay had already achieved. Also Audsley, though he was raw, had, as his subsequent career testifies, a real talent. Like Gale Tattersall, prize-winning cameraman on *My Ain Folk*, and like many others, Audsley found working with Douglas extremely educative. Indeed, both as a director and as a teacher, Douglas had a superb ability to educate; that is, to draw out from people latent ability and perception. Audsley, like Tattersall, went on to work on *Comrades*, and his description of editing with Douglas confirms what we already know of the perils and potentials of such a task:

> Bill was not, I later realised, his own best editor. Often he couldn't see the strengths, so often could not quite spot the weaknesses. He found it hard to step back because being such an intuitive, emotional creature he needed someone else to look over his shoulder. His writing had this mixture of incredible sparseness and then these incredible jumps. We used to draw out sequences on paper and do these little drawings. His footage was often a nightmare to cut because it combined these longueurs and stillnesses with the most abrupt moments. In fact he told stories with emotional rhythms and not the 'action' rhythms of most cinema. I had to learn all this and also learn to respond to Bill's intuitive response to what you were offering him. We never sat and *talked* about these things. Like painting a room, he could recognise it when you offered him what was the image he had sitting at the back of his mind. Until these rhythms were absolutely perfect he was completely at sea. He could not move down the film until he had got each stepping stone pretty much fixed.

Audsley also thought Douglas could go off at destructive tangents in editing – a destructiveness equal to his creativity – but that this was generally avoided. Destruction, however, did arrive from an external source. Douglas's initial concern about the imperfections of the soundtrack turned to panic and outrage as, inside the BFI, chaos was caused by an attempt to lay the soundtrack on what Mingay was to allege was a wholly inappropriate 20-track system.

Superficially, the row that followed resembled that over the editing of *My Ain Folk*. The difference was that on this occasion Douglas was not exaggerating minute issues out of all proportion: the soundtrack was radically flawed.

In October 1977 Douglas, in tears, approached Mingay who, well beyond the call of duty, agreed to recreate the proper soundtrack. This was a longer, more expensive task than he had originally thought. On 14 March 1978, however, he wrote to all members of the Production Board and the BFI's Board of Governors summarising his view of how Douglas and he had been treated by Sainsbury. He pointed out how difficult it had been to elicit £76.75 legitimate expenses (£51.30 was finally paid, ten months late) at the time his work had earned £7,000 from the German TV contract. He noted how he had been dropped after this and that any attempt to contact Sainsbury was met 'with hostility and insults from Nita Amy, who was a stranger to me'. Mingay continued:

Bill Douglas re-approached me in October 1977 with reports of artistic disaster, and the collapse of relations with his producers. I felt bound to do my best to finish successfully a project in which I had a hand.

He had obviously suffered at the hands of incompetent and inexperienced producers. The film showed signs of amateur cutting and misconceived dubbing. A great deal of money had been wasted. I understood that Sainsbury could no longer communicate with Douglas, and that I had to work through the intermediary of Judy Cottam. Douglas offered me £200 out of his future profits as payment, and was obviously in a very weak position personally to secure the artistic integrity of his conception of the film. He was intolerably battered by the treatment he had received from Peter Sainsbury. Every effort had been made to force him to deny his instincts about the state of his own film.

If the investment of the film were to be secured, he desperately needed a period of support and uninterrupted concentration after the making of the film had been so diluted over many years of personal hardship. He had received no benefit from the favour of earning his own budget by producing a premature television version.

As I feared the sheer destructiveness of a mid-term approach to Sainsbury and Amy, I advanced the cost of further dubbing sessions in an attempt to complete the film without further disturbances, to meet Festival deadlines, and to reduce the cost of interrupted concentration.

In consequence Mingay bypassed Sainsbury and approached Michael Relph. After a viewing paid for by Solus, Relph, according to Douglas, admitted that the Board knew the former soundtrack was unacceptable and confirmed the film greatly improved. With the soundtrack corrected, Douglas 'was able to dare to see that he had errors in his cutting of sequences in three reels' and was able to solve these problems. Mingay further noted that although it was known to officers of the Board that he had accepted the task of correcting the soundtrack from October 1977 to February 1978, no acknowledgment of his existence had been made. He was also, once bitten, concerned about the Board's response to the expenses he was incurring. Financial stringency slowed both him and Douglas down as the latter 'worked slowly towards a recovery of artistic control, and really needed several stages to recreate the true dramatic thread of the film.' Sound-wise Mingay considered the film a shambles:

The film as I discovered it had been surprisingly little altered from its

German-version stage, in the picture, and then track-laid with twenty tracks per reel, a great deal of poor post-syncing, and the removal of many original tracks. The dialogue had been brutally filtered. Bill Douglas's films receive their impact from simple original sound, dramatised by well-chosen exaggerations. He was a stranger to this amateur version of *Lawrence of Arabia*-style work, and had relapsed into total silence on the soundtrack in rejection of what was being foisted on him.

Two sessions used up the £700 and a further £300 lent by John Kobal. (Actually included in my invoice details.) I had been dragged into a great deal more work than originally envisaged before I saw the scale of the track laying. I had, for instance, to reduce by huge labour the twenty tracks to a manageable number. Succeeding sounds were spread in arbitrary patterns across the range of empty tracks. This is virtually undubbable. It is also a massive task to reduce to manageable proportions.

I have explained the reasons why I distrust Sainsbury's 'filling' of invoices. He also seems to like to use one person against another. He knows nothing of track laying, laboratory costs, industry practices, industry manners, or of the responsibility of employers. He avoids consultation. He is rarely at his office. He is totally uninterested in the technique of film-making, and is unable to discuss or judge its problems. In low-budget work this is the essence of success, as the costs of dubbing, laboratories etc. are the same to all-comers. Yet a film has to bear comparison with others on a much higher budget.

The Board makes a few 35mm films, and obviously seriously mistakes the budgeting of them. It is ludicrous to compare the costs of 35mm with 16mm. For instance, theatre viewings are a necessity (not a luxury) in 35mm, unlike 16mm.

I have grossly undercharged my work. And I have saved costs by all my actions, where others have squandered money. I have brought this film to the point where its investment is safeguarded.

We are talking, of course, about what is ultimately government money, and the way it is being administered. The case history of this film must cause concern to those in higher authority over these funds.

I hope the Board today will be able to guarantee the payment of my invoice, and thus facilitate completion of the film. There may still be time to make it one of the few British representatives in the Cannes Film Festival, and to re-launch the entire Bill Douglas *Trilogy* in the most commercially successful way.

The film did make Cannes, attracted interest and, back in London, had a prolonged, highly successful run at the Academy Cinema. The London, European and North American reviews were excellent. The films were sold to the BBC for showing in 1981. Other distribution and TV deals, however, fell through. Douglas, supported by Cottam and deeply in debt, was critical of BFI sales and distribution methods past and present. He noted, for example, that the rights of the first two parts of the trilogy had been given to the Australian Film Institute for nothing.

It is impossible to judge whether, if the Production Board had at that point been enthusiastically supportive of the trilogy, a different distributive and hence fiscal outcome could have been achieved. Even with Hassan's energetic ambition for the first two films, the BFI had to operate within constitutional, fiscal and logistical constraints which seemed to preclude real wealth generation. What is certainly happily true, however, is that BFI Production after Sainsbury reverted to Hassan's policy of making two or three low-cost feature films rather than twenty shorts. Terence Davies, another Hassan initiate, is Douglas's successor. Colin MacCabe, when Head of Production, saw it as an imperative that BFI films should reach a cinema audience. Regrettably, however, when Douglas's *Confessions*, a script combining the popular and the innovatively profound, came before the Production Board it was rejected. Sadly, the story of Douglas and the BFI had no happy ending.

INTRODUCTION

How ironic it is that Bill Douglas should start work on his film script about the Tolpuddle Martyrs in 1979: the very year that Margaret Thatcher's election as Prime Minister heralded a fundamental change in British political and social ideology. Over the next decade her government was systematically to undermine not only the trade union movement in Britain, but, more significantly, those values which had inspired Douglas in the first place, in favour of an ethos of selfish individuality and acquisitiveness. *Comrades* was finally released in August 1987, two months after the Tories had triumphed at the polls for a third time in succession. That the morality of *Comrades* should be so out of kilter with the climate of the time may partly explain why it has not had the cultural impact (particularly in terms of the audience it has reached) that such a rich and inspiring piece of contemporary cinema deserves. For it is true to say that *Comrades* remains an undiscovered film for many, its critical and cultural resonance far less than that of Douglas's celebrated *Trilogy*.

The making of *Comrades* was a particularly painful and frustrating process. Not only did it take Douglas eight years to get his film made – including one false start in 1984 when a crew and actors had been hired only for the plugs to be pulled at the eleventh hour – but the production ran substantially over budget, was subject to a lengthy and fraught editing process, and finally, despite favourable reviews, achieved extremely limited distribution.

One frequently expressed opinion is that Bill Douglas was a film-maker working in the wrong place at the wrong time: that his highly distinctive and personal cinematic style was frustrated by the institutional practices and the dominant aesthetic concerns of 1980s British cinema. In the production of *Comrades*, the question of artistic control (and unrealised or thwarted achievement) frequently crops up. This question influences assessment of the film, *as a film*. Everything meaningful or interesting about a film cannot, however, simply be reduced to the individual personality of the film-maker. These issues affect understanding of *Comrades* in another way: too often discussion has been concerned with the film 'which might have been' rather than the film which was seen by the public.

'COMRADES': A PRODUCTION HISTORY

After finishing his *Trilogy* in 1978, Douglas was invited to teach for a year at the National Film School in Beaconsfield. During this period the need to make another film, something which would take his professional career beyond the realms of autobiography, inevitably arose. His ideas for possible scripts included three Scottish subjects: a Life of Robert Burns, an adaptation of James Hogg's novel *Confessions of a Justified Sinner*, an idea based on James Boswell's journals; and two other possibilities which were ostensibly English in subject matter: the life of the playwright Joe Orton, and a project based on the story of the Tolpuddle Martyrs.

The idea of making a film about the Martyrs came about when Douglas picked up a pamphlet recounting the story of the Tolpuddle men while on a visit to Dorset in the late 1970s. However, his major source of inspiration (and information) for the script was a volume entitled *The Martyrs of Tolpuddle 1834–1934*, published by the TUC in 1934 to commemorate the centenary of the arrest and transportation of the men. Additional sources of material included a pamphlet written by the leader of the Tolpuddle men, George Loveless, entitled 'Victims of Whiggery' (the final speech made by George Loveless at the end of the film was constructed from sections of this pamphlet), and copious research notes by Peter Jewell on a variety of relevant topics including traditional English folk songs, the way of life of rural farm workers, nineteenth-century agricultural practices and midwifery!

With the cast of *Comrades*
DAVID APPLEBY

The script of *Comrades* was completed by the summer of 1980. Douglas had secured a commission of £7,500 from Mamoun Hassan at the National Film Finance Corporation on the strength of the first twenty pages of completed script, rather than the usual treatment or story outline, which Douglas resolutely refused to do throughout his career. The script was regarded by many who read it as a highly accomplished piece of work. One reader for the NFFC, Stanley Reed, who had championed *My Way Home*, made the following comments:

> I ... find myself astonished by the intensity of the writing and the vividness of his conceptions, which extends to every detail of character, action and settings.... The script promises a film of deep humanity and high imagination, powerfully felt but controlled by a rigorous mind; few film-makers attain this degree of concentration – one thinks of Dreyer, Buñuel and Bresson.

Douglas's poetic writing style, demonstrated forcefully in the published screenplay of *Comrades* (Faber and Faber, 1987), found many admirers, including Jeremy Isaacs of Channel 4, who was impressed by the fact that it was 'written in imagery ... as a film should be written'. Actor Alex Norton, who was to play a major part in the film, had a similar reaction. He describes the writing as 'magical ... it was like watching a movie in your head'. Douglas conjured up a series of vivid images which carry and advance the narrative in an almost seamless, organic fashion. This is particularly true in the Dorset sequences, which elegantly establish the characters within a wider framework of social , economic, political and personal relations. In contrast, the Australian sequences are episodic, short filmic essays imagining what might have happened to each man in turn.

Douglas tells the story of the Tolpuddle men in emotional and human terms. He is more interested in relationships – between the characters, between individuals and their environment, and ultimately between ordinary people and society – than in plot. This is why he chose not to show, for example, the trial of the men but rather to focus on their wives and families, huddled pathetically together in the court corridor, barred from witnessing the injustice which was to deprive them of their husbands and fathers for several years. The spare, taut dialogue reinforces the sheer economy of his style. Essentially a writer/director, he formed his cinematic concepts while sitting at his typewriter. He spent a year writing the script for *Comrades*, refining the narrative and the characters until he knew he had exactly what he wanted. As he told me in 1988:

I have to feel the thing as I write it out. I go over and over it again until I know it back to front. When I go to sleep I run the script in my mind both forwards and backwards. At the same time I'm actually trying to visualise how we'll see the thing happening.

The subsequent problem was always how to get these images, which obviously burned with a great intensity in his mind's eye, up on the screen. This was to prove as difficult in the case of *Comrades* as it had been in the production of the *Trilogy*.

One particularly interesting feature of the script was the creation of the figure of the Lanternist, who appears throughout the film as different characters. Each manifestation of the Lanternist coincides with the depiction of an optical device or effect. Douglas had an obsession with pre-cinema, what he described as the 'marvellous optical entertainments invented by showmen and scientists on their way to discovering cinema'. Some of the characters are essentially enter-tainers like the Lanternist himself: Sergeant Bell and his Raree Show (a character taken from a 1839 print), the Diorama man in the John Bull waistcoat, the Witch at the phantasmagoria. Others are pioneers – the mad Italian photographer,

Alex Norton as the Lanternist
DAVID APPLEBY

C19th travelling lanternist by Gavarni
BILL DOUGLAS AND PETER JEWELL COLLECTION

artists, the silhouettist – or are devices to introduce further optical effects: McCallum (camera obscura), Wollaston (flicker effect with cards), the Sea Captain (moving toy panorama), the tramp (Roget's optical illusion), the Ranger (thaumatrope), the usher (shadow theatre), and Mr Wetham (the *trompe-l'oeil* picture 'Blossom and Decay'), a character cut from the final film. Even the three-directional picture which James Loveless shakes his fist at in Frampton's house features a portrait of the Lanternist as the 'Laughing Cavalier'.

In addition to commissioning the script, the NFFC financed a visit to Australia to allow Douglas to find suitable locations. He had already scoured the Dorset countryside to find a village to stand in for a Tolpuddle now become too modern to be considered. After visiting 130 villages he settled on Tyneham, an abandoned village in the middle of the Army firing range at Lulworth. However, raising money for the project proved difficult, and little progress was made over the next two years. Part of the problem was the lack of a producer. Mamoun Hassan, who had made a substantial commitment to the budget of *Comrades* (estimated at around £2 million), had approached several notable British producers, including Otto Plaschkes, Simon Perry, Clive Parsons and David Puttnam, but they had all turned the project down. Richard Craven, who produced the Scottish segments of *My Way Home*, was linked briefly with *Comrades*, as was the production company Portman Quintet, but neither connection materialised into anything concrete.

Progress started to be made in late 1983 when Channel Four, by then rapidly becoming one of the major sources of funding for British film-makers, became involved. Jeremy Isaacs was not only enthusiastic about the script but was also sympathetic to the themes of the film, which he regarded as appropriate material for the Channel: 'I thought that the values the Trade Union movement had stood for at its best and noblest, the values that informed a more humane and just society than Margaret Thatcher stood for, were the values we should espouse in our films.' He persuaded the Channel Four Board (who had to approve any expenditure of over half a million pounds) to allow him to put £1 million into *Comrades*, the largest single investment Channel Four had made at that time.

This involvement led to the appointment in early 1984 of Ismail Merchant as producer. Merchant was a major force in the industry with many films to his credit, mostly made in collaboration with director James Ivory. As Jeremy Isaacs saw things at the time, Merchant was just the kind of producer the film needed:

Ismail is an operator of the first order. It was apparent that even with a budget of £2 million it was going to be extremely difficult to bring the thing in on budget. Ismail was pretty good at cutting the corners in film-making – enabling him and James Ivory to make the movies they did for budgets that astonished other people.

Douglas himself had first met Merchant at a film festival in Bombay ten years previously and had been given a copy of a novel by Ruth Prawer Jhabvala (another close collaborator of Merchant and Ivory), *The Widow*. In order to keep working while waiting for *Comrades* to happen, Douglas had recently completed a first draft of an adaptation of the novel for Merchant, for which he received no payment. Unfortunately, their collaboration was to prove a disaster. Disagreements began to arise in relation to central aspects of the production of *Comrades*, including the script, the budget and the schedule. Merchant sent the script to Jhabvala, who clearly had many problems with it. He subsequently wrote to Douglas, pointing out that Jhabvala found it 'hard to understand', the personalities of the six martyrs 'undefined', and disliked what she saw as the preponderance of 'cloying cute kids'. Jhabvala also felt that the story really did not get going until the first pay-day scene. This opinion reveals a set of narrative priorities quite different from those of Douglas, as this scene happens after several crucial sequences which set up the social relations in the village and the major sites of struggle. Merchant obviously shared Jhabvala's reservations, and this failure to understand and appreciate Douglas's vision was to doom the collaboration.

Financial problems also arose. Merchant had approached completion guarantors Film Finances Ltd with a script, budget and schedule in order to secure a completion bond for the production. The role of the completion guarantor is to ensure, for a premium, that any budgetary 'overages' will be covered by a completion bond. The company had problems with the script and the budget and were reluctant to give a guarantee. Merchant also used this hitch to force Douglas to condense parts of the script, in order to reduce the British schedule to six weeks (Douglas wanted seven weeks in Dorset) and save some money. Douglas resolutely refused to make any such changes.

In spite of these fundamental disagreements, the film was cast, a crew hired and a production start scheduled for the beginning of October 1984. Meanwhile, relations between director and producer deteriorated further. Douglas resented Merchant's sacking of the original designer Allan Barrett and his attempt to impose his own composer on the production, despite Douglas's wish to have Hans Werner Henze. While most producers would expect the right to collaborate with a director on such decision-making, Douglas's insistence on meticulous control over every detail of the production, coupled with his mistrust and, by this stage, intense dislike of Merchant, made the situation intolerable. Two weeks before shooting was scheduled to start on 1 October 1984, Douglas made it obvious in a letter to David Rose at Channel Four that he could no longer work with Merchant: 'Clearly he has no faith in me or my script, and I now certainly have no faith in him. ... This man has downtrodden everything along the way with never a positive word to say to anybody on the film.'

The start of the film was subsequently postponed, with Merchant and Douglas blaming each other. What is clear is that Merchant, for whatever reasons, delayed confirming the postponement to cast and crew. Robin Soans, who was to play George Loveless, had rejected a job at the Royal Court after being reassured that the film was going ahead as planned. He later discovered that the producers knew the film was to be cancelled but were reluctant to release the information. Meanwhile, Jeremy Isaacs and David Rose attempted to patch things up between Douglas and Merchant to save the film. This process dragged on, with very little enthusiasm on Douglas's part, until November 1984 when relations between the protagonists had failed to improve. Douglas again wrote to Rose: '... it is quite pointless to pretend that this production is feasible with Ismail in charge. It is altogether too late and I sometimes wonder whether Ismail himself really wanted the film to be made at all. Certainly not with myself as writer/director.' Channel Four decided then, as Isaacs puts it, to cut their losses and Merchant was subsequently paid off, for an allegedly greater sum than Douglas was ultimately paid to direct the film.

That year, the 150th anniversary of the original events in Tolpuddle, certainly seems to have been the lowest point of the entire process for Douglas. However, a new producer was quickly found by Isaacs and Rose in Simon Relph, a respected industry figure who was on the verge of being appointed Managing Director of British Screen, the semi-privatised body which replaced the government-funded NFFC when it was disbanded in 1985. Relph had earlier been approached by Merchant to see if he would be interested in co-producing the film, but this offer had later been withdrawn. He was determined that history would not repeat itself – particularly in having cast and crew believing that the project was going ahead when in reality this was not the case. So a careful time-plan was drawn up, stipulating certain arrangements be made by certain dates before actors and crew were contracted. The schedule was tied to the time of the year, with autumn/winter required for Dorset and summer in Australia. This time the organisation was properly handled by all concerned and shooting began in Dorset on 1 September 1985.

The budget by now had risen to around £2.3 million. Rank had previously

considered investing in the film with Merchant as producer but had withdrawn interest when he left the project. The commitments from Channel Four and the NFFC were still in place but a further investor had to be found. As neither of these two parties was guided by straightforward commercial motives, they were able to grant a favourable position, in terms of recoupment, to a third investor, and the British distributor Curzon subsequently came up with the final portion of the budget.

Douglas and Relph had gathered together a strong cast and crew. Cinematographer Gale Tattersall and editor Mick Audsley had both worked with Douglas before and were sympathetic to his working methods and personal vision. But the casting of the film was particularly interesting. It was always Douglas's intention (when it became clear very early on that he would not have recourse to non-professional actors as he had done in the *Trilogy*) to cast virtually unknown actors to play the Tolpuddle men, their wives and families, and to use more famous artists – 'the aristocrats of their profession' – as the upper-class characters. In this way, the casting strategy paralleled the relationships in the story. The rationale for using such an approach was that Douglas did not want anything to get in the way of the portrayal of George Loveless and his comrades:

> I didn't want a Robert Redford standing in for George Loveless because I knew the audience would see Robert Redford and I wanted them to see instead the glory of this man. So I wanted actors who would be humble enough to want to share the same experience in presenting these men. When I came to the aristocrats it wasn't a terribly difficult decision because it really didn't matter if the audience felt a division between the character they were looking at and the person playing the character.

Douglas found his 'unknowns' largely through the skill and insight of casting director Susie Figgis, who understood his obsession with finding the right faces to fit the parts of the Tolpuddle men and their families. One interesting footnote here is that Douglas cast veteran actor Alex McCrindle, who had been in the original production of Miles Malleson's play *6 Men of Dorset* in 1934, in the role of the Gaoler.

Shooting finally began in Dorset on Monday 9 September 1985 and at first things went well. Although Douglas had a reputation as being difficult to work

Previous page: The men of Tolpuddle await their meagre wages
DAVID APPLEBY

with, the atmosphere on set was relatively relaxed and productive. Robin Soans, for one, found working with Douglas an extremely interesting and enriching experience. He quickly understood Douglas's concern to omit any spurious 'acting' from performances which would get in the way of emotion, and was able to bring that understanding to the role in a very effective way. Douglas had explained to Soans the importance of physical stillness, coupled with intense emotional activity which, if sincerely created by the actor, would shine out of his eyes. Soans noted how different the atmosphere on set was compared to the usual situation on a feature film:

> Film is a very rarefied medium. A lot of the time the product seems secondary to the whole process of making films – the most important question is 'Where are we eating tonight?' or 'What wine are we going to have with the salmon?' This film wasn't like that – or at least most of it wasn't like that. The people who lived that sort of existence seemed out of place. ... The lack of selfishness and the degree of goodwill (on the part of the actors) was quite astonishing and must have been very similar in its own parallel way to the community spirit which must have existed between the Methodist labourers at the actual time.

This situation changed somewhat with the arrival of the aristocrats, particularly Freddie Jones and Robert Stephens. Up to that point, Soans argues, they hadn't really been in the world of acting but rather of recreating the Tolpuddle of 150 years previously. All of a sudden they found themselves in a big house with 'actors' making a lot of noise and being very self-important. Significantly, Douglas had problems controlling both actors, and this unfortunately shows in the rather overblown and caricatured performances they give in the film.

Alex Norton, who was cast as the Lanternist, points out that Douglas did not give the actors a lot of direction as such. He worked in terms of the larger frame and, as a result, neglected the nuts and bolts of how a character should move, whether he or she should walk out of a shot at the end of a take and so on. Norton had problems with this at first, noting that his first day on the set was 'the worst start of any movie I've ever done'. In the end, however, Norton regained his confidence by seizing the initiative and even occasionally improvising both actions and dialogue – the only actor in the film who was allowed this degree of freedom. A great trust was subsequently built up between Norton and Douglas, and Norton found his performances going from strength to strength as a result. Norton was subsequently Douglas's ideal choice for the role of the demonic Gil-

Martin in *Confessions of a Justified Sinner* but was not considered bankable enough.

The problems with the production intensified in Australia when the film began to go over-schedule and over-budget. Part of the difficulty was the extremely bad weather. The film had been scheduled to set up a strong visual contrast between the greyness of autumn in Dorset and the sunshine and dazzling light of an Australian summer. What happened was the opposite: an Indian summer in England and rain rather than the brilliant sunshine expected in Australia. But Douglas was also unfamiliar and unhappy with some of the Australian locations. One example noted by Simon Relph was the orange grove location where Young Stanfield's story takes place. This turned out to be not at all what Douglas had imagined (disrupting his working method, which involved having everything worked out in his head beforehand) and he found it a difficult sequence to shoot. As Relph explains: 'It would have been much better if we could have contrived a situation which, when those things happened, he could simply have stopped, rethought it and come back the next day.' Obviously with a tight schedule and a full feature cast and crew on location this was not possible. The outcome of these problems was that the Australian shoot, which had been

Squire Frampton (Robert Stephens) and the Vicar (Freddie Jones): the villains of the piece
DAVID APPLEBY

scheduled to last four weeks before Christmas 1985, ran over into the new year, precipitating a real budgetary crisis.

These problems obviously affected Douglas. The threat that the film might be stopped caused him great anxiety and frustration and sapped his enthusiasm. The pressure was by now also being felt by cast and crew but, as Alex Norton points out, the actors had begun to discuss privately the possibility of working for nothing to get the film finished: a demonstration of their great commitment to the project and to Bill Douglas. Relph admits that things were always going to be rather tight in Australia and that perhaps more care should have been taken over the preparation of the Australian budget. Luckily the resulting 'overages' were partly covered by the completion guarantors, but the investors also had to contribute to allow Douglas to finish the film the way he wanted – shooting what was left in relation to the script rather than hacking the schedule and leaving the problems to be patched up at the editing stage – otherwise this would have been limited by the terms of the bond. Principal photography was finally completed in January 1986, with some subsequent pick-ups back in Britain.

The next problem was the editing. This process took much longer than expected, and developed into a series of arguments between the director and his financial backers which primarily concerned the length of the film. *Comrades* was the first film Douglas had made which was edited as it was being shot. With Mick Audsley, he produced a version of the film which ran for 3 hours and 25 minutes. This was considered too long by the principal investors, particularly Curzon, the film's distributors, and Jeremy Isaacs. The question of length had always been a problem. Simon Relph notes that there had been a worry in the beginning that the script was too long but nothing was done about it. But in any case Douglas was not prepared to compromise his vision. Jeremy Isaacs wrote to Douglas that virtually all of the middle section of the film 'should be cut and will not be missed'. He wanted it to be shorter and tauter because it would then have a much better chance of reaching a wider cinema audience.

Wishing to remain true to his vision, Douglas attempted to resist these pressures. Exhausted after months of hard work, coupled with the expected departure of Mick Audsley, who was contracted to begin work on Stephen Frears's production *Prick Up Your Ears*, he reluctantly gave in and began a process of shortening the film. He gave way on several significant things, including the positioning of the interval which he had planned to happen after the men had been thrown into prison, integrating the break into the overall structure of the film as scripted. The backers wanted the interval to occur between the English and Australian sections of the film – which is what happened. Channel Four made a cut of the film on video, without Douglas being present, to demonstrate how it could be shortened, but the result is rather messy and, significantly, not all that shorter at around two and three-quarter hours. Douglas worked with Mike Ellis, who had been personally approved by Audsley, and produced a revised version of about the same length as the Channel Four cut, which was premiered at the 1986 London Film Festival. The film was enthusiastically received and won an award for the 'most original and imaginative' film premiered at the National Film Theatre during the year.

Douglas had signalled in a letter to Simon Relph that he was not fully satisfied with the cut shown at the London Film Festival, feeling that they had 'ended up with a hybrid version forced on us by the pressure to make the film shorter' – a feeling strongly shared by Mick Audsley. However, the strength of the plaudits received after the festival screening persuaded the film's financiers to allow some final alterations. So yet another editor, Simon Clayton, was appointed to help Douglas restore around eight minutes of material to the film which had been cut from the original 3 hours 25 minutes version. This final cut was shown at the 1987 Berlin Film Festival and released later that year.

While he feels that this final version is the best of the four cuts mentioned,

An image: the men carry the chairs up the hill to Frampton's . . .
DAVID APPLEBY

Simon Relph points out that the film was still too long: 'I think the reason we never really found precisely the right film is because Bill didn't understand the necessity of trying to get it down a bit to something that could be screened more widely. He was constantly battling against the idea of losing things.' But Relph also acknowledges that Douglas had worked out everything so thoroughly while writing the film that to remove anything effectively upset the balance he had achieved in his mind. This is supported by Mick Audsley, who understood fully the finely structured ellipses in Douglas's narrative and the echoes which occur throughout the film. To remove one brick in the wall affected the whole.

Comrades was finally released in August 1987. It played for only six weeks in London at the Curzon West End (despite opening to extremely good reviews). Ironically, it came top of a critics' choice poll for 1987 in the *Independent*, beating films like John Huston's *The Dead* and David Lynch's *Blue Velvet*. While audiences were good for the first couple of weeks, attendances then began to drop dramatically. Roger Wingate of Curzon notes that word-of-mouth publicity for the film was not particularly good, and he subsequently decided, in spite of Curzon's heavy investment, not to continue with the film in the West End and to put it into another Curzon cinema once its fixed-term booking had come to an

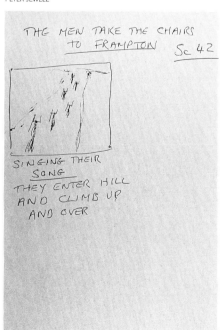

. . . and its inspiration: Bill Douglas's storyboard
PETER JEWELL

end. As Simon Relph points out, the film did well in art-house cinemas but not in mainstream venues. Overseas distribution was also very poor. It was sold to Australia, Germany, Spain and Italy for small amounts of money and failed to find a distributor in France and the United States. Relph insists that Bill Gavin, the sales agent, promoted the film strongly but, primarily because of the length, very few people were interested.

To date, *Comrades* has been screened twice on Channel Four. First on 27 April 1989 to an audience of 1.9 million, then, six months after Douglas's death, on 23 December 1991, this time with 1.3 million viewers. It is now rarely seen in the cinema, and only two prints exist in Britain.

A CRITICAL REASSESSMENT OF 'COMRADES'

The production history of *Comrades* is a stark demonstration of the tensions and struggles which lie at the heart of the film-making process. It highlights the problems of what is an individual and a collective endeavour at one and the same time, raising fundamental questions of creativity, control and ownership. In Douglas's case, these questions arose most forcefully in the relationships between the film-maker and his financiers. As Simon Relph says of Douglas:

> Like a lot of great artists I think he genuinely expects the people who had the money to give it to him and allow him to do what he wanted. The fact that they wanted to be involved or that they wanted to criticise or influence the content of what was happening was always something he found difficult to take. The truth is they gave him a tremendous amount of freedom in what he did.

Robin Soans takes a rather different view:

> So many of the people who have power in the industry want to be seen to have some influence on the artistic creation of a film without the knowledge

The director and his producer Simon Relph on location in Dorchester
DAVID APPLEBY

or the understanding required to do that. With someone like Bill they are going to meet a brick wall because it's his own intensely personal vision of life which is being made, and nobody else really has a place in that. Even the actors – although we created and gave of our own emotions – we were very much in Bill's hands. It was very much *his* film. It wasn't our film. He maintains the balance of power within the film he wants to create.

Despite the protracted difficulties, Douglas made his film, not exactly as he wanted, but closer to the vision set out in the script than many of those who were urging him to shorten it might have wanted. Indeed, what strikes one immediately when reading the shooting script is exactly how much of it is up there on the screen. The issues of collaboration cannot be dismissed altogether, however, in that while Bill Douglas effectively created his films at the writing stage this was not done in total isolation. The advice, criticism and suggestions unselfishly provided by Douglas's companion Peter Jewell supplied the vital sounding board which he needed while crafting his ideas. Consequently, I would argue that Jewell's role as script editor on *Comrades* was significantly more important to the undertaking than has been acknowledged. I also feel that the contributions of Gale Tattersall, whose skill helped Douglas transfer the images in his head on to celluloid with such searing clarity, and Mick Audsley should not be underestimated. Indeed Douglas valued the work of both very highly.

Returning to the question of technique, what Douglas achieves in *Comrades* is a rendering of what he called 'emotional narrative', concentrating on characters and their relationships rather than plot as such. Everything is stripped down to the bare essentials. There is no visual clutter (none of the obsession with 'correct' period detail which marks so many British films), no unmotivated camera movements or optical trickery for its own sake. This style is fundamentally shaped by Douglas's profoundly humanist perspective, and his belief in the basic goodness and nobility of ordinary people. Which, as Robin Soans explains, helps us to understand the stillness of many of the images:

When a character is in dilemma – which he portrays better than anyone else you can think of in the cinema – you have to see that process happening. Bill makes films about things we all go through, we all have these dilemmas. Because it's so simple and so moving – there's just a window, or a wall, and two figures – one is confronted with an absolute relevance to one's own life. And you can't rush that.

This accounts for Douglas's concern with moments, small gestures, expressions, simple events such as the breaking of bread. These images for him are the very stuff of cinema and reveal far more than accurate reconstructions of great events and a plethora of detail. This is the opposite of the approach associated with the liberal humanist epics of David Lean and Richard Attenborough which are packed with 'big' scenes featuring thousands of extras.

Also of interest is the basic morality of the film which, despite the subject matter, is less political than religious. In a private note to himself Douglas described the film as 'a political subject but not political in intent. I do see it as a religious experience.' Certainly religion is of central importance to the film, with the opposition of Church of England and Methodist chapel used as a means of understanding the social and political structure of England at the time, with the former preserving the hegemony of the aristocracy and the latter functioning both as a site of non-conformism and resistance and also as a community to provide mutual support in the face of economic depression.

The structure of *Comrades* falls into two parts. The Dorset sequences mesh together to form an organic seamless whole. Douglas did not like the idea of discrete scenes and preferred to construct a narrative which flowed more like a

George Loveless (Robin Soans) on his way to transportation
DAVID APPLEBY

musical score, a unified elliptical structure. The narrative links and recurring motifs ('echoes' as Douglas called them) in this construction are fundamental to the unity of the whole – hence his reluctance to cut sequences at the editing stage. The film begins with stunning images of machine-breaking and retaliation by the forces of law and order, viewed by the Lanternist on his way to Tolpuddle. It continues in this richly visual way, depicting the good people of Tolpuddle at work and prayer. Douglas also brings in the parable of the six chairs, which functions as a metaphor for the six martyrs. When George Loveless persuades John Hammett the carpenter to ask the landowner Frampton for more than the agreed price, the chairs are promptly returned. The next time Loveless asks Frampton for too high a price, it is not chairs but people who are at stake.

The Australian sequences, on the other hand, are constructed as separate episodes, although even here there is an attempt to link them through the characters of Charlie and Fop. These episodes are themselves an echo of the work scenes where each Martyr is seen labouring in the fields, and are designed to demonstrate the ambiguity of the Australian experience which embraced alternately over the six episodes both the repression and brutality of life as a convict and the 'good life' represented by the new world. As Douglas himself acknowledged, the irony

George teaches Charlie (Symon Parsonage) the meaning of comradeship in Australia
DAVID APPLEBY

of the Martyrs is that in Dorset they were free yet enslaved, and in Australia they are prisoners but find freedom. The original plan was to shoot the Australian sequences in Panavision and have the cinema screen open out, but the centrality of television funding made this impossible. However, Douglas did attempt to signify the sense of freedom and space represented by the Antipodes by utilising off-screen sounds for the first time in the film, alluding to space beyond the frame. In Dorset all natural sounds had been constrained within the frame.

Despite his absolute belief in the power of the image – 'I always think that an image is stronger in the end than anything that anybody can say' (BFFS Film Supplement no. 4, 1988) – sound is extremely important in *Comrades*. Douglas had decided early on that he wanted Hans Werner Henze to compose the music for the film, after witnessing his accompaniment to a screening of Stroheim's *Greed* in Brighton several years previously. What impressed Douglas was the fact that Henze was prepared to leave sections of the film entirely silent, using his music sparingly and to maximum effect, an approach which would suit his own predilection for natural sounds. As Douglas noted in one of his fellowship lectures at Strathclyde University:

> You may recall Hollywood using music to sugary lyrical effect in the accompaniment of the flight of natural birds in *Out of Africa*. … Henze … appreciated fully the natural sounds of things and never wanted his music to compete. To his ear the flapping of the bird's wings would be beauty enough.

The recurring themes in Henze's marvellous score skilfully augment Douglas's visual links and echoes which proliferate throughout the film.

Douglas's aesthetic approach in *Comrades* embraces techniques already familiar from the *Trilogy*: the use of stillness, of composition, of the construction of simple images which encapsulate fundamental emotions and meanings. These are derived from a particular philosophy both of the world in general and of the image in particular. Douglas's concern for the nobility of ordinary people is manifest not only in his choice of subject matter but also in his whole approach to cinema:

> I'm very admiring of what the camera can do. The camera can reveal a great deal without words. It can reveal the inner soul of people. If you rush through words and rush images you don't get into the heart of human beings. In life I remember there were moments when I sat looking at people

when they were in repose, and there was a beauty about them, and a stillness. And when I came round to look through a camera perhaps one was looking for that moment in life.

This philosophy bears a striking affinity with some of the ideas of the great French critic and theorist André Bazin. Bazin championed film-makers such as Stroheim, Murnau, Dreyer and Flaherty as exemplars of a cinema which 'rejects photographic expressionism and the tricks of montage' and instead turns its attention to revealing the reality of the world. The following quotation, which refers to Stroheim, demonstrates what I mean:

> In his films reality lays itself bare like a suspect confessing under the relentless examination of the commissioner of police. He has one simple rule for direction. Take a close look at the world, keep on doing so, and in the end it will lay bare for you all its cruelty and its ugliness. (From 'The Evolution of the Language of Cinema' in Mast and Cohen [eds.], *Film Theory and Criticism*, 3rd edition [New York: Oxford University Press, 1985], p. 128.)

The chain gang turn on their brutal overseer
DAVID APPLEBY

But the aesthetic concerns of Bill Douglas cannot simply be reduced to Bazinian concepts. He is also interested in the effects of montage and is clearly influenced by Soviet cinema, as several critics have pointed out. However, what is especially interesting about *Comrades*, and the reason why it should not be overshadowed by the *Trilogy*, is that while it represents a continuation of Douglas's interests in the rendering of truth through the image, it also explores very different, even contradictory, questions of cinema as artifice and illusion.

This later interest arose partly in relation to the different set of institutional arrangements operating in the production of *Comrades*. Unlike the *Trilogy*, which featured several non-actors in major roles, this film had to be much more conventional in terms of production practices. One consequence was that Douglas, for union reasons, would have to cast professional actors in all the major roles, despite his stressed preference for working with non-actors. However, once he had reconciled himself to this constraint, he developed a fascination with the craft of acting and, more precisely, the artificiality of this craft. Douglas explores this in two ways in the film.

Firstly, the casting structure had implications for how characters were read by the audience, as I have noted above. However, despite great sincerity and skill on the part of the actors, particularly those portraying the Martyrs and their families, Douglas's own dictum that 'Actors (tend) to be too well looked after' compared to non-professionals who have 'the problems of life on their face . . . life seems to leave its marks, and they don't seem to be over-concerned with removing or covering them' was borne out. The faces of the men and women of Tolpuddle (with a couple of exceptions) simply weren't etched with the pain of experience which was so palpable in the *Trilogy*.

More radical and successful is the creation of character through the Lanternist and his deployment through the film. Douglas's idea that the story is actually told through the eyes of the Lanternist – the sub-title of the film is 'A Lanternist's Account of the Tolpuddle Martyrs and what became of them' – sets up an interesting parallel between Alex Norton's character(s) and Bill Douglas the film-maker. The film is consequently rendered a cinematic *interpretation* (rather than a reconstruction) of historical events, the implication being that the film-maker's craft is one of illusion, in much the same way as the Diorama man recreates the battle of Waterloo, or as Douglas himself brilliantly utilises a diorama to depict the actual transportation of the men. What it amounts to is a bold acknowledgment of the artificiality of cinema. By casting the same actor (recognisably so) in all fourteen parts, Douglas ruptures the realist coherence of the narrative, introducing a character analogous to a 'common man' or a Greek chorus figure. The

Lanternist also embodies most literally the concept of transformation which was central to Douglas's concerns in the film. To him, this was a film about transformation: of individuals and of history itself (the beginning of the labour movement), all rendered through the illusions of optical devices.

Douglas develops his strategy in other ways. The film begins with a burning white light – which appears to be the sun, subsequently eclipsed by the moon. The film ends with a similar image which this time is identified as a circle of light cast by a projector, prompting a reassessment of the meaning of the original image. What Douglas has constructed is a neat framing device which self-referentially marks the enclosed narrative as a film. In this way *Comrades* is as self-reflexively aware of its own status as a fiction as classic modernist works such as Bergman's *Persona*, which begins with two carbon arc rods coming together to form the light of a cinema projector and ends with them being pulled apart, a strikingly similar device to that used in *Comrades*.

The transparency of the text is also disrupted on several occasions when characters directly address the cinema audience by looking straight at the camera, a device used to great effect in some of Godard's early works and most notably in British cinema by Tony Richardson in *Tom Jones*. In *Comrades* it is used three

The Martyrs: free and reunited
DAVID APPLEBY

times: the silhouettist, the knowing look of the Lanternist on stage at the Old Vic ('It was almost as though he had been present throughout himself'), and when James Hammett comes out of the wages shed and holds seven fingers to the camera. The effect of this direct address is rather unsettling because it disrupts the relationship between the spectators as unseen onlookers and the film, confronting the former with their relationship to what they are watching on the screen.

So at the heart of *Comrades* lies a reconciliation of two opposing philosophies of cinema: a realist Bazinian philosophy of the medium as a 'window on to the world', and a self-reflexive acknowledgment of its artificiality. In this, the film grapples with the fundamental properties of the medium of cinema. Above all its other considerable merits, this achievement marks *Comrades* as a major contribution to cinema. It deserves to be recognised as such.

Along with genuine feelings of personal sadness and loss, there can be detected, in much of the writing and talking about Bill Douglas since his death, the distinct tones of institutional guilt. Typically it is covered over by anecdotes of his intensity or his obsessive inability to compromise, or by a curious celebration of the impossibility of working with the man on the set; but underneath the anecdotes lurks the guilt. The obsession and the impossibility become the marks of a peculiar genius which the British film industry wasn't big enough to handle or to find a place for. Douglas becomes a convenient symptom in which can be traced the failure of British cinema to invent and sustain an art cinema, and a convenient stick for the ritual self-flagellation with which the industry periodically consoles itself.

The record clearly calls for some explanation. Almost twenty years of filmmaking produced three short films, *My Childhood*, *My Ain Folk* and *My Way Home*; one very long one, *Comrades*; and a great deal of pain and frustration with projects which everyone admired and no one would fund. Unerringly, Douglas's career seemed to head towards the gap which the industry could not fill: the gap between, on the one hand, the intensity and condensation of the short film made with minimal resources, and, on the other, the magnitude and epic reach of the long historical drama. What flows into this gap, and what is sometimes mistaken for the British art cinema, is the 'English quality film', defined by production values and characterised by a melancholic nostalgia for classes and values caught at the moment of their disappearance: a film industry marching hand in hand with the heritage industry. What is missing between the important but marginalised work of the experimental, political or workshop sector and the soft-focus 'images for export' of the quality cinema is a sustained, hard-edged and diverse *European* tradition of art cinema. Bill Douglas, particularly in the *Trilogy*, seemed to point towards that; but, failing to meet the primary requirement of British film investment – that images should be designed to sell in the English-language market – he could not sustain it and the industry could not sustain him.

The industry, deprived of the kind of public support which any art cinema requires, has an excuse. Closer to my own academic home, and perhaps less excusable, there is room for a shadow of guilt too. Mistaken when the films first appeared as yet more British humanist realism, the *Trilogy* slipped through the theoretical and political net with which many of us trawled in the 70s. Too individualistic to point to film as a social practice, and too realistic to open the way to the avant-garde whose absence had always (has always) deformed British film culture and whose advent was eagerly awaited after the events of 1968, Bill Douglas escaped the attention (he may have been relieved) of the academic study

Don't Mourn – Analyse: Reviewing the Trilogy John Caughie

of film which was rising as he was making his early films. He did not figure in the debates about realism on which much of that study was based. His name does not appear in the standard academic collections on British film history; it appears in one line as one of a list of film-makers and films in Roy Armes's *Critical History of British Cinema*; and, to the best of my knowledge, he was never written about in the standard academic journals. He was reviewed at the time, even championed, by Derek Malcolm, Philip French and others, but he avoided academic canonisation and the mixed blessing of becoming a good teaching text.

Again, Douglas hit a blind-spot around art cinema of academics who were also radical intellectuals. The cinema on which film theory cut its teeth was the popular Hollywood cinema of the classic period in which the ideologies of a whole social, political and economic culture could be seen on display, and caught out, sometimes, in disarray. There was an urgency of engagement with the popular, with its contradictions, and with the pleasures which it offered as its rewards. The European art cinema, on the other hand, was stigmatised as the address of individual genius to a social elite. Film theory in the 70s chose as its object the institution of cinema rather than the uniqueness or excellence of individual films. This is not to renounce the work of a critical theory which I would still defend as foundational for the academic study of film or television, but to recognise the blind-spot which it created, and which made it difficult, in Britain in the 70s, to *see* the cinema which Douglas's *Trilogy* pointed towards.

Speaking from home again, you could expect this of English film-makers, critics and academics – but in Scotland? While Bill Forsyth started a 'school' of Forsythean comedy, the 'school' of Douglas has not been copied, far less developed. In 1982, when a group of us tried to build a polemic to attack the debilitating traditions of kailyard and tartanry, we 'forgot' Bill Douglas. In my own teaching, it wasn't until – somewhat as an afterthought and very belatedly – I showed *My Childhood* on a double bill with Terence Davies's *Distant Voices, Still Lives* that I realised what a central film it was. For Scottish culture, we can now see, Douglas's *Trilogy* stands in the same necessarily destructive relationship to the filmic kailyard tradition as the anti-kailyard novels of Hay and Brown stand to the more comfortable kailyard literature of Barrie and Crockett. What we took then for an individuality which placed Douglas – excellent but eccentric – on the margins of Scottish film culture can be seen now to place him in a central Scottish cultural tradition which had simply not been represented (and has not been represented since) in Scottish film: a cultural tradition, moreover, which links Scotland to some of the great Northern European traditions. It is precisely this which gives a sense of cultural loss to the failed project of Douglas's adaptation of one of the most powerfully European texts of Scottish literature, *The Confessions of a Justified Sinner*, a script which could not be funded during his lifetime but which, with almost predictable irony, may become fundable after his death.

Confession is, of course, good for the soul. The guilt that underpins the sense of loss at Bill Douglas's death, however, could simply perpetuate the lack of critical engagement with his work, allowing him to remain an obsessive misfit or a marginalised genius, and failing to grasp the productive unease which his work creates within the more secure traditions of British film culture. Don't mourn, analyse.

There is a scene in *My Childhood* which seems to stick in the visual memory. It is the scene where Jamie heats a cup with hot water, empties the water out on to the table, and presses the warmed cup into his Grannie's frozen hands. More precisely: Tommy, the older brother, has brought a bunch of dead and drooping flowers from his mother's grave. The scene opens with a close shot of the flowers in a cheap china cup sitting on a table whose furrowed grain echoes the textured wood which figures throughout the film. In the second shot, Jamie, the younger brother, the central character of the *Trilogy* and the bearer of Bill Douglas's autobiographical investment, enters frame left. Entrances from the edge of an empty frame are a feature of Douglas's style, formalising the structure of the scene and establishing the space as place. (The film is composed of scenes rather than sequences, framing relationships rather than developing actions.) Jamie crosses to the table carrying a heavy kettle of boiling water, picks up the cup and tips out the dead flowers on to the floor. This is all a single shot, with a very slight following movement, lasting about twelve seconds. The third shot is a medium close-up static shot, framing the cup, the kettle and, at the edge of the frame, Jamie's torso. His arm reaches into the frame; he picks up the kettle, pours water into the cup till it overflows, and then keeps pouring as the water spills all over the table. Still within the same static close-up shot, he picks up the cup and empties it on to the table, shaking out the drips. All we have seen of Jamie in the shot has been his arm and part of his torso, and as he withdraws from the frame the camera lingers for a moment on the kettle: it and the cup have occupied the central space of the frame. In a relatively quick long-shot of the Grannie's room – bare boards, empty grate in the black-lead stove, furniture broken up and wallpaper stripped to provide fuel for an occasional brief fire – Jamie crosses and kneels in front of his Grannie, who is dozing in her rocking chair, bundled up, a black shape in the particular contrasty black which characterises the film, only her white face and hair emerging from her shawl. A cut into big close-up of

Jamie's hands and Grannie's hands, a symmetry of composition; Jamie pushes the warm cup into his Grannie's numb fingers, closes her hands around it, holds her hand in his, patting them gently. Fade to black; end of scene; there has been no speech.

I am straining under the delusion that to describe a scene is to convey its meaning and effect. It isn't, of course. The scene takes about forty seconds, implying a condensation and concentration which description dissipates. But perhaps on the basis of the description something can be said about the scene which may open out on to how the film works, and the *Trilogy*, and why we need to understand Douglas better. Following the Soviet montage stylists whom Douglas admired (Donskoi in particular), the scene, like the film as a whole, is built in blocks which exist in dialectical rather than causal relationship with one another. The film is a montage of scenes and frames, read backwards and forwards in relation to each other, rather than a linear narrative leading to resolution and closure. In many instances, a change in the order of the scenes might damage the rhythm but it wouldn't change the narrative. At the level of the scene, each block has its own shape, held characteristically in the film in a static camera or a still composition: a still life. The cup of dead flowers, for instance, stands at the beginning of the scene quite precisely as a parodic still life, linking this scene to the scene a few shots earlier of Tommy at his mother's graveside. Placed thus, the opening image imports into the scene in rigidly condensed form the whole intense net of family relationships and misrecognitions: Tommy's dead mother, Jamie's mad mother, Tommy's father who is not, as Jamie thought he was, the same person as Jamie's father. When Jamie empties the dead flowers on to the floor, then, it is not simply a functional action, it is a symbolic gesture within that missing and confusing narrative.

The gesture of emptying out the flowers in the first shot is repeated in the next shot with the spilling of the water and the emptying of the cup. There is a kind of senseless untidiness in these gestures, a wilful messing of one's own space, which shocks my bourgeois sense of domestic propriety. What they do is crucial for the film's effect: they mark off this poverty as 'other'. Poverty is presented not simply as a deprived version of everyday norms – the same but less of it; poverty appears rather as a system which has learned to develop other norms and other rationalities: poverty as a peculiarity which is not simply given. The formal discipline of the scene excludes any sentimentality, but admits a kind of dull, accustomed pain. The meaning of the scene, its rationality, only appears when Jamie presses the warmed cup into his Grannie's hands. Characteristically, the meaning of the scene does not refer simply to a particular version of the familiar, cannot be read along the lines of generic or cultural coding, but is built out of concrete bits of the peculiar, lived experience of poverty. In that sense, scenes have to be read backwards, the wilful spilling of water only cohering with the warming of the hands. In that sense also, many scenes have a surreal quality – Grannie wandering, distracted, in the fields with a dead crow wrapped in paper – the surrealism of memory fragments which do not hang together.

Like actions within it, the scene itself is gestural rather than narrative in the very precise sense in which Brecht and Benjamin talk of the *gestus*. It condenses a complex experience and a social and familial context within a highly formalised single action. Its formal restraint and understatement leaves it to the spectator to complete the statement, an image of poverty seen 'as if for the first time'. Far from having anything to do with the British realist tradition, Douglas is working within the aesthetics of distanciation developed by Russian formalism: an aesthetics which owes very little to the repertoire of forms which film theory associates with Brecht, but a common source out of which Brecht also developed his theory and practice. The estrangement or distanciation which the formalists speak of is a strangeness which allows us to see the everyday as if for the first time. It is precisely the condensation of this little scene which casts poverty as strange, quite 'other', and quite unsentimental.

A moment of stillness and reflection: Stephen Archibald on the set of *My Childhood*

But it is not simply about aesthetic distances. The scene ends with tenderness, Jamie's hands enclosing those of his Grannie, gently patting them and warming them before the scene fades to black. Images of tenderness are rare and fleeting in the film, and unanticipated within the surrounding desolation. A few scenes earlier , after a bitter fight between the two boys, there is a long shot across the room of the backs of the three members of the 'dysfunctional' family, sitting round a fierce, brief fire. The shot is held till, just before the cut, Tommy's arm creeps round his younger brother's shoulder. The quick cut prevents any lingering on a moment of unexpected closeness. It was only on second viewing that I noticed it. In the last part of the *Trilogy*, *My Way Home*, there is a scene of Jamie and Robert in a rare moment of pleasure in the nonsense routines of National Service which ends with an abrupt cut at the point at which Jamie has put his head against his friend's shoulder. It is almost subliminal, and again I had to replay to make sure that this moment of physical affection had taken place. The almost obsessive reticence which underplays these moments is not prurient – not a coy allusion to a love that dare not speak its name – it is simply uncertain: a fragility within the films around the possibility of sustaining relationships. And yet these glimpsed moments ground the films emotionally, opening them to complex possibilities rather than burying them in easy despair.

Aesthetic distance and intense intimacy, then, is the dialectical tension which marks the *Trilogy*. Bill Douglas seems to me to stand between the formal and visual rhetoric of silent cinema, particularly Soviet silent cinema, and the psychological intensity of the best of European art cinema. It is perhaps his Europeanness which made him so hard to recognise as Scottish in the early 80s and which makes him now so important for Scottish and British cinema. Surrounded by a great deal of blank, marketable International Style quality cinema, both in Europe and in Britain, endlessly recovering a lost past, Douglas's films seem to offer one possibility of an art cinema which is built from the experience of locality, and from difficult and insecure histories.

Two other things seem to distinguish the *Trilogy* from most British productions: silence and anger. Douglas created meaning on the image track, leaving the audience continually to complete it. This is the 'pure cinema' which Truffaut called for in the 50s, the absence of which in Britain led him to believe that 'British cinema' was a contradiction in terms. Built on the foundation of a long, powerful theatrical tradition, British narrative cinema tends towards the felicities of script and dialogue rather than towards the symbolic and expressive images of Hollywood or the best of European art cinema. For Douglas, speech is as gestural as the image, telling us little, alluding to a lot. Meaning comes after the image, is never simply given in it. It is this which makes the films 'difficult', resistant to instant psychology.

The silence – the absence of a connected discourse which might give you an easier access to the experience of the characters – is not simply formal. Within it, there seems to me to lie an unstated anger and grief at the hardness of poverty: an anger about the deprivation of memory and of the past which is absent from the gentler nostalgias that are now being constructed, and was never there in so rooted a form even in the loudly stated 'Angry' films of the 60s.

These are the characteristics which seem to me to distinguish Douglas: a gestural condensation, an absence of sentiment about the past, a stark lyricism of imagery, and an elliptical and expressive silence which can refer either to deep anger or to buried tenderness. They are qualities which seem to be absent in the English quality films of the 80s: films which draw on a great tradition of the English novel from the 19th century through James, Forster and Waugh, but which forget, in a rapture of exportable soft focus, the sharp irony which gave that tradition its edge. They seem trapped in their Englishness both culturally and economically, selling a pageantry of the middle classes in an English-speaking market. Douglas seems to me to belong in a Scottish cultural tradition which has access to the cultures of Northern Europe. This is the possibility which his *Trilogy* opens for a Scottish cinema in particular, and why it seems important to understand it.

I have said very little about *Comrades*. This is not because of any antipathy or lack of interest. Much of what I have said about the *Trilogy* can be said about *Comrades*, which, despite its length, is a work of considerable condensation. What *Comrades* adds is a lyricism around the land and a good humour without which grimness could become simply a Scottish house style, the perpetuation of cultural Calvinism. But for the purposes of this essay, it is the sharp, condensed formality of the *Trilogy* which crystallises for me what is so distinctive about Douglas, and what is worth recovering in his work for a British art cinema.

It still seems possible to value many of the priorities and commitments which were cherished in the political excitement of the 70s, priorities which made it easy then to marginalise Bill Douglas. It still does not seem naive to me to want an Other Cinema, a cinema of social practice, of diversity, of the avant-garde. In order to value Bill Douglas it should not be necessary to revoke the past or retreat into collective guilt. Nor should it be necessary to invent a Bill Douglas who will accommodate that guilt by occupying the position of auteur, genius or prophet without honour. The questions which Douglas's career raises are material ones as well as aesthetic ones, infrastructural as well as cultural, and to relax into the celebration of lost genius is to dodge the hard questions and allow it all to happen again. Within the realities of the new audience for cinema, the new conditions of production, and the new map in which cinema circulates, it does seem necessary to consider the possibility of a mainstream British art cinema, an art cinema which we do not yet have. Douglas's work seems to me to be one of the key indicators of a possible British or Scottish art cinema equipped with a hard enough edge to cut through the bland cinema of nationalist nostalgias and clever ironies, or the 'made for television' cinema of production values and quality quotas.

To end with mythology and the personal. I had heard the anecdotes of the Black Douglas in production: obsessive, compulsive, dictatorial, suicidal when he did not get his way. What I was not prepared for when he ran a series of scripting workshops for our postgraduate students was deference, patience, self-efface-ment, gentleness and immense generosity. It is that generosity that this piece is in some sense meant to repay. But the gap between the two images also says some-thing about the films. Public anger and private gentleness; formal obsessiveness and delicacy of feeling: a dialectical tension which British cinema, if it ever had it, is in the process of losing.

(An earlier version of this essay appeared in *Sight and Sound*, vol 1, no 7, in November 1991.)

I was already biting my nails at the age of five, chewing into them till they bled. My earliest memory is of me crouched below the kitchen sink watching my father, an AA veteran, scoop handfuls of green and yellow capsules into his mouth from a clear plastic tub he hid in the top cupboard. Often, panting milky breath, I'd peer through a button-hole in my mother's maroon raincoat, watching her slapping him over the breakfast table. Like most kids I knew, I spent my formative days under coats, within dens and in among the long grass – hiding from my dad.

Irvine was to be Scotland's last New Town, conceived in the late 1960s as a uniform nirvana fresh off the Danish blueprints, offering the Glasgow overspill inside toilets, jobs as assemblers in Japanese computer plants, and regular buses to the Costa del Saltcoats up the road. As a boy, I cut a daily path through cement mixers and stacks of chipboard, running across the forbidden main roads and over wooden bridges ready for demolition, to lie in my favourite place: a soft field in a place called Bogside. It was more of a clearing, I suppose, between a geriatric home on one side and a training farm for boys with Down's Syndrome on the other. I stretched out on the grass, chewing my hands, reading about the lives of American movie stars in large-format colour books. While I lost myself in Garbo's laugh, Lombard's crash or Marilyn's fatal affairs with the Kennedys, the explosives factory along the coast, at Ardeer, would let out a mighty bang. Every afternoon, between 12 and 3, it grumbled and burst like an erupting ulcer in the belly of the community.

I found out years later that my field in Bogside was the site of an extinct mining village called Bartonholm. The dusty patch from where I'd watched the transformation of these Ayrshire villages, and pored over my star biographies, was the same one where children from earlier days had crowded under the pithead of the famous Bartonholm mine. An old man who knew the place told me that the children of the village were well known for making strange herringbone patterns, like storyboards, with their feet on the whinstone paths during dry summer days.

When I decided to write about the films of Bill Douglas, I went back to the old Bartonholm clearing to get my bearings. Many had died in the village, by accident or through pneumoconiosis, and when the pit closed the families lost their company cottages and were given houses newly developed in the nearby town. As I walked back from the fields, I thought of how my own growing awareness of small-town life had been given a painstaking visual language in the films of Bill Douglas. It was an awareness of broken promises and crumbling illusions – both inside my home and outside, in the shambolic 'ideal corporate living space' that was the Scottish new town. Scotland, my own imagined community, had produced an artist who mocked the quixotic posturing of a bogus national identity – exploding the tired, iron platitudes of family loyalty, couthy neighbours and yer ain fireside – and who transformed the historic antagonisms of his country into the flickering shadow-play of great cinematic art.

In his *Trilogy* Douglas had sought to express the pain of a lonely, neglected childhood in a world where the decline of heavy industry, and a way of life, deepened the confusion. It's something many of us recognised, it's an old Scottish story, but rarely does Scottish art open out so fully to the nuances of such change as in these films. I didn't know any children like David Balfour or Peter Pan, our cultural child-heroes, but I've known many who buzzed glue or did drugs or ran away or went into adulthood damaged by family hatreds and lack of opportunities. These facts – small, embarrassing perhaps – are part of what makes Bill Douglas's films connect with our towns, our decline, our language and the contradictions embedded in our experience as a nation. Beyond this, his work has the capacity to break with our traditional sense of nationhood, offering a cinema which can make itself meaningful in a global context.

My Childhood opens with the voices of schoolchildren singing that sterile paean to divine grace and providence, 'All Things Bright and Beautiful', in the local school. Out of the grey emerge the two central figures in the *Trilogy*: Jamie, the boy, and Newcraighall, a small mining village bathed in white light and studded with coal and slagheaps. Jamie is completely silent for the first twenty minutes of the film. A quiet aria of shots and cuts establishes the depressed conditions of the village and the wantonness of the boy's care. He lives with his elder brother Tommy under the somnambulant shadow of their dying grandmother. Looking like the dark witch in a thousand fairy tales, or one of Dostoevsky's horror-stricken peasant women wrapped in her rough and soiled *drap de dames*, their whimpering grannie suffers in silence the accumulated resentment of the boys' confused parentage. In one scene, after a vicious scrap between the boys, the 'family' of three crowd round a smouldering flame gasping in the grate. Slowly, in a strangely shocking moment of tenderness and pathos, Tommy stretches his arm over the back of the chair and places it lightly on Jamie's shoulder.

At their best, like early films of the silent era, Douglas's films can seem to draw the very heat out of your body as your eye makes its way to the centre of these saturated, meditative moving pictures. A turbulent well of mystery and memory is stirred and turned over somewhere at the back of your eyes as you follow the rhythms of light and shade, sound and silence, which constitute Douglas's vision of Newcraighall. Jamie's early steps towards a consciousness of family hatred and poverty are cut with images of coal men emerging from the pithead and vehicles struggling over a land that seems pitted against them. In this way, the legacy of animosity and cruelty within his immediate family (chiefly a psychological pressure) is matched with the physical brutality of the land, and the human effort to subdue it and traverse it. Both are hard taskmasters; both succeed in isolating and depressing Jamie. He craves love and care, not revenge. He wants to paint the land, not cut into its seams. These twin pressures are eventually enough to make Jamie wish he was dead. His mother in an asylum, and his good grannie buried, the last scene in *My Childhood* shows Jamie dropping himself from an iron railway bridge onto a coal wagon passing underneath. He sits among the coal, staring back towards the source of his grief, whilst being transported along the line that might deliver him from Newcraighall.

Running away from home is a kind of painful, ritualistic adventure for many children, but never had it seemed so essential, or to offer such promise of deliverance, as when Jamie drops onto the coal wagon. You can never be sure whether this drop is one inspired by thoughts of permanent escape, of suicide, or whether it fulfils a desperate need in the child for mere physical passage from the village and his miserable life there. No matter: the scene itself and the lyrical succession of images which precede and justify it are so strong as to explode effectively the fanciful mythology which has long held sway in romantic tales of Scottish childhood, family and community.

Douglas's *My Childhood* was premiered at both the Edinburgh and Venice film festivals in 1972. It won the Silver Lion at Venice and almost caused a walk-out in his native city, where many thought it 'boring', and 'an insult to his own people'. John Gibson, of the *Edinburgh Evening News*, wrote, 'You'd think it could never have happened here, as close as Newcraighall on the edge of Edinburgh. It's so austere, so depressing.' Helen Crummy, a local woman who played the part of the schoolteacher in the film, felt that the people from Newcraighall had hated it. 'The local people who had known Bill as a boy felt guilty on seeing the film. They thought the film showed the community to be uncaring,' she said. Lindsay Anderson, however, felt that Douglas had something special, calling him 'a poetic film-maker, whose feeling for moment and the intensity of the image makes him unique.'

Set in the mining village of Newcraighall, on the eastern outskirts of Edinburgh, the production of the films, like the miners' cottages themselves, was under threat of subsidence from the start. In the same year as the first film the local newspaper ran the headline 'LEASE OF LIFE FOR DYING VILLAGE', with the news that the community was to be saved from demolition. A longstanding Newcraighall resident told me that many in the community felt that Douglas had betrayed them. He'd painted an unflattering portrait of the small community which many found insulting, especially at a time when the town was undergoing a period of 'renewal'. On reading the original script, the parsimonious lips of the Films of Scotland Committee had clamped tight at the idea of the films. Dismissively, they raised a bureaucratic finger: 'Not a penny!' It seems they were excitedly producing *Cumbernauld: Town for Tomorrow* at that time. These people shared the desire for 'positive' images of their town, their country, their culture. Yet the economic malaise and cultural torpor that Douglas brings into focus in the films is as relevant to the present-day political situation in Scotland as it was to his own austere childhood. It attempted to show how the living conditions of working people, and the lack of opportunities for economic improvement, were a constant in these communities. Ten years after *My Childhood*, Newcraighall was in the midst of a long, doomed battle against McGregor's pit closures.

The *Trilogy* concerned itself mainly with the struggle of a child against the poverty and mental cruelty of a mining village in which opportunities for economic and cultural growth were non-existent and where people seemed proud and pious as a result of their difficulties – resistant to change rather than desirous of it. *Comrades*, however, is concerned with a group who attempt to beat the system which keeps them down. The film was made during the Thatcher years, a time during which the very ethos of trade unionism was under considerable attack and when the practices of union organisation, the capacity for unions to take effective action in industrial disputes, were systematically diminished in a series of bills steam-rollered through Parliament. *Comrades* was completely antithetical to the spirit of the times in which it was made. In the way it shows the Dorset workers moving from self-awareness to solidarity (through persecution) to final vindication, it provides an ironic commentary on these times and is full of a hope and faith in the collective power of people in overcoming adversity which was not only lacking in Thatcher's Britain but, interestingly, in Douglas's earlier vision of his home community.

Douglas's place in world cinema is guaranteed by the way he infuses social minutiae with imaginative light, with a keen eye for technical and artistic invention. In *Comrades*, his use of the camera obscura and the diorama – his practical re-telling of pre-cinematic development – serves as a metaphor for the Martyrs' increasing perception of truth. Douglas knew, like William Blake, that poetical vision, the fine deployment of the imaginative eye, is akin to freedom, to a species of political emancipation. The Lanternist's tale of the Martyrs' arrest and deportation depends upon the notion of illumination, both technical and philosophical. Douglas's way with the camera, and his self-reflexive aesthetic, links him with film-makers like Tarkovsky, whose similarly lyrical revelations of creative processes, social change and the aura of humanity (in films like *Andrei Roublev*, 1966) are among the best we have.

Douglas does not shirk, however, emotional elements for the sake of objectivity, in the way that some of the Russian masters do – Eisenstein and Tarkovsky among them. In this respect he reminds me of Robert Bresson, whose compositional genius and ability to convey austerity and spirituality with tranquillity is very like Douglas, especially in the *Trilogy*. Bresson had a compulsion to show 'what is happening inside'. His films have been called 'remote', 'cold' and 'depressing' (much like Douglas's), but Susan Sontag has argued that 'one has to understand the aesthetics – that is, find the beauty – of such coldness ... there are spiritual resources beyond effort, which appear only when effort is stilled.' By looking hard for such spiritual resources in the human face, in a dark village, in a home without comfort, in the midst of cultural distraction, Douglas's films show remarkable vision. Like Bresson and like Vigo, Douglas attempted to imbue found situations with a disciplined formal intelligence – and thereby to look at them in a new way. All three often used non-actors; eager to avoid overbearing exterior 'expression' and 'acting'. Douglas, though, did use professional actors to represent a 'class' of people: the authorities. In *Comrades*, where workers are often unknown, the clergy and boss class often have famous faces and voices – an effective , though not unproblematic, way of influencing the viewers' sympathies. By using non-actors to convey noble feelings and admirable characteristics in the workers, and professionals to represent the overblown, degenerate characters of the upper class, Douglas overturns more than one stereotype of Shakespearean actorliness and causes us to look at these types anew.

The opening sequence of Vigo's *Zéro de Conduite* (1933) is an important precursor to Douglas's kind of film-making: two boys blowing up balloons on the train, impervious to the camera, framed from below, their movements and the shape of their balloons caught in perfect light and contrast. Douglas shares this magical ability for composition. Despite the shortness of his film career, Douglas is deserving of comparison with some of the most original world cinema talents. His cinema has influenced directors such as Terence Davies, whom he taught at the National Film School when he was there for a short period between films. Davies's own *Trilogy*, as well as *Distant Voices, Still Lives* and *The Long Day Closes*, bears a similar relation to elements in European cinema which have hardly affected the mainstream British cinema.

The Los Angeles *Times* called Douglas's *Trilogy* 'arguably the finest achievements in narrative film to arrive from Britain in at least a decade'. By eschewing devices which promote easy (or complacent) narrative flow, and by avoiding starchy explicatory dialogue, Douglas moves toward a kind of emotional mimesis. The narrative, though chronological, consists of a subtle patterning of scenes, composed like independent structures or still lifes. The syncopated movement of the scenes builds towards both dramatic and emotional combustions; a rhythmic visual story-telling which avoids the often dramatically programmatic uses of camera and sound in contemporary cinema. The concentrated, monochromatic gaze of his camera, at the centre of which often lies an expressive stillness, is such that viewers must look to the juxtaposition of scenes and the musical dynamics of cutting to follow the story. Like a traditional oral ballad, the films demand that you enter into the formal rhythm of the shots. In order to complete the syntax, the viewer must imaginatively leap back and forth across scenes as across lines of verse. It is ironic that the style of these films should bring the oral ballad to mind, for Douglas's films constitute a critical assault on the cultural tradition that draws much of its force from the Kailyard.

My Childhood chokes on the Scottish grand lie of hearth and home. Child-like innocence is a luxury foreign to Jamie. He is spared none of the more brutal shocks of a family gone awry and an industrial community in sharp decline. A cruel parallel between his own fate and that of the broken spiritual nomads around him is seen as he stands beside the hospital bed of his insane mother. Seeing him, she pulls the sheet wearily over her head. Later, curled into a ball of foetal confusion, in his Grannie's cottage, he repeats this gesture slowly and with a searing inevitability. Douglas attempts to reassert the expressive truths of personal experience and historical fact, whilst scorning the trite wishful-thinking of the cabbage patch. Romantic nationalism and the High Kirk have, for almost three centuries, bombarded Scottish culture with clusters of sentimental, God-fearing solvency. Like the backward and pathetic Cree Queery (who sings 'Ower the Watter for Chairlie' to his sick mother to make her think he's happy) in J. M. Barrie's 'Cree Queery and Mysy Drolly', the Kailyard son is as daft as he's good-looking: always able to suffer hardship and penury with a half-glad smile – a ridiculous Calvinist masochist who makes a virtue of his own servile, blunt consciousness. When he dies of 'getting a good meal from a friend of his earlier days after being accustomed to starve on potatoes and a very little oatmeal', we are surely forced to ask ourselves what unbridled havoc this sort of nonsense has wreaked on the cultural health of the nation, let alone that of other nations packed to the gunwhales with belated men of feeling. Having been brought back to the village, in *My Ain Folk*, Jamie is again turned away by his selfishly promiscuous father and forced to live with his grandmother on his father's side. Forever the fearful, Calvinist self-denier, she sees Jamie as a product of his mother's deranged, immoral nature: 'Your mither ruined ma son's life.' Shot mostly with her back to the boy, the old woman sits endlessly brooding in front of the fire with the dog on her lap and Jamie at her back, under a table. Above him, on the worktop, sits a bowl containing an apple and a set mousetrap. Such are the small, expressive miracles Douglas creates that many of the objects situated in the frame look preternaturally solid. Like objects in Vigo's *L'Atalante* (1934), milk bottles, apples and a glinting knife seem to have an essential corporeality seldom seen on film.

For the old woman, bent and racked as she is with animosity, Jamie's one saving grace is that he's his father's son. When drunk and duly sentimental, she strokes and intoxicates *him* with boozy affection. 'Oah, ma darlin' . . . ma young prince,' she says. We remember that her prime term of endearment for her son is 'king'. Like the murderous dynamics in Ibsen, we learn that the father's saving lie may be the ruination of the son. Jamie, however, desperate for kindness in any form, later whispers quietly in bed, 'Please Jesus, make ma grannie drunk every night.' Not for the first time has a Scottish child – or any child where drink defines the rhythm of their day – discovered they prefer a kiss through breaths of whisky to a smack from the sober palm.

Any ambitious ideologue hoping to subdue the minds of the Scottish people could have no firmer ally than the educational establishment. Like the cultural Kailyarders, their unspoken remit has traditionally been to close the mind to contradiction and open it to the glorified dominion of God and the government. It's not such a recent thing that for many kids the gulf between school and a good job looks wider than that between school and prison. Longrigend, that hellish borstal and temple to the monumental deficiencies of sectarian schooling just outside Glasgow, claimed a couple of my schoolmates and just about cornered my own brother. I lived in a borstal myself, but as an inmate of a slightly different kind, when my father got a job in one. Living in a dungeon masquerading as attached staff housing, I would often meet and talk with boys gone crazy with misunderstanding; their various childhood traumas having given way to endless advice from neurotic, disaffected social workers, sessions with drunken psycho-analysts with the sensitivity of rottweilers and a regular round of corporal punishment and 'short, sharp shock' if they failed to comply. Of course, some of them were just plain bad, even helpless. Mind you, I don't remember ever meeting one who was as sick or unstable as my own father, who regularly drove their bus on the open road. When Jamie is taken to the children's home by Tommy's father, the cruel absurdity of these institutions is brought comically into focus. Tommy, responding typically well to the convivial environs of the institution, immediately starts dipping his father's pocket as he sits down next to him on the bed. Triumphantly, he offers him back one of his own cigarettes. Though a comically subversive moment of payback for the boys, who laugh their heads off, it is clear by the end of the scene that there will be nothing for Tommy. The most he can hope for is the army. Jamie's passage to a home is inevitable. As the dark van which takes him there climbs up a steep Edinburgh brae, a sham army of pipers and drummers in full romantic regalia pass down the hill on the other side. Irony breaks into agony as the tartan-clad warriors of a self-deceiving nation – gone in the teeth, dead in the head – strike up the savagely irrational 'Scotland the Brave'. Scotland's search for a noble identity, as ever, means nothing more than the ceremonial waving of a blank banner and the collective aversion of eyes from prevailing, indigenous social injustice. Edinburgh cracks open before our eyes.

From the banal imperial dementia of the Tattoo down to the tartan-mad rows of shops on the Royal Mile selling lines of mythical Caledonian simulacra, Edinburgh has long been the site of a romantic nationalism gone awry. Walter Scottism, and an infected Balmorality, has turned it into a city rife with cultural terrorists and kilted bureaucrats: a schizoid town which so foregrounds the illusionistic that you might easily forget the complex matrix of unemployment, disease and drug abuse which lies beneath its bonny civic weaving. The Upward Mobility, rich from parental investments in public relations and glass-blowing, attend local crammers on the 'Reel of the 51st Division' and the 'Gay Gordons' before zooming northwards to the Angus Private Subscription Dance or the Perth Hunt Balls. This is the paradoxical face of a city full of antique charm masking disease and poverty. The crisis of cultural representation in Scotland is not answered by the home-rulers, struggle as they may to convince that the solve-all is independence. Edinburgh – the 'Athens of the North' and all that that means – would stand at the centre of this Disneyfied little state as out of touch with real people and existing social concerns as it is possible to be. The green worm of nationalism helps Scotland to turn inwards, to fortify the borders of both mind and habitat and to revel in illusory escapolitics. Bureaucrats clutching rigged calculators would stand beside tartanised landlords – a reckless junta born of hard times and galloping sentiments – united in their effort to reinstate what Tom Nairn has called a 'decrepit presbyterianism and imperialist thuggery'. Increases in the quantity and quality of power centred in Edinburgh over Scottish affairs now seems essential. The paralytic cry from the advocates' bar, however, like that from the terraces of Hampden, must be revealed for the xenophobic banter that it is and expunged from serious discussion of how to improve the economic self-determination of the country. That way lies a federal Europe and a national culture free of essentialist dogma and historical fantasy. That way lies a more genuine independence.

Only when Jamie escapes from Scotland, once conscripted and sent to Egypt in *My Way Home*, does he move towards a sense of hope and burgeoning creativity. An awakening to a world beyond the successive 'homes' he has encountered as a child – befriending a genteel Englishman and seeing Arabs in conditions and states he can identify with – brings him to a more pluralistic conception of the world and his place in it. By homing in on something universal, Jamie breaks the homogeneous impulse; he ruptures the walls of that parochial sense of value-in-belonging which, after his childhood experience, he knows to be an idealistic lie. Whether dressed in alien kilts, as he was at the Home when play-acting, or wrapped in the drunken arms of his spiteful Grannie, the younger Jamie is revealed as a child oppressed and mistreated by his 'roots'. Without Helmut, his German friend, Jamie at home had been like the abandoned kite they once flew joyfully together: lonely, insecure and drifting. In Egypt, Jamie sees other worlds, other cultures, within which he can find acceptance after Scotland's rejection of him: worlds of the imagination, of reading and collecting books, of making films, of experiencing exotic religions and possible love between men. In the end, he has come out to embrace his own, open, ambivalent identity – in a way that runs counter to the traditional values and supposed certainties of his Scottish roots. By opening his mind and applying his imagination, he has found his way home, a way which leads in the opposite direction from the religious pieties and cultural prejudices he left behind. In the last scene of *My Way Home*, an aeroplane engine can be heard as the small rooms of Jamie's childhood come into view, bathed in a translucent whiteness. Jamie, at last, like many of us, has had to leave home to home in on himself.

Home is both beginning and end for many Scottish artists. A vigorous literary counter-tradition includes George Mackay Brown, Edwin Muir, Alasdair Gray and Liz Lochhead, who have tried, in their various ways, to rip open the myriad shibboleths of cabbage-patch and tartan-mongering. Ian Hamilton Finlay, in sculpture; Stephen Campbell, in painting; and Elspeth Gardner, in ceramics, have also examined myth, form and tradition in relation to Scotland's social and cultural history. It is purely in terms of Scottish cinema, and images of Scotland constructed in films made outwith Scotland, that Bill Douglas's *Trilogy* is discovered to be something of a loner. His critical intelligence, the uncompromising

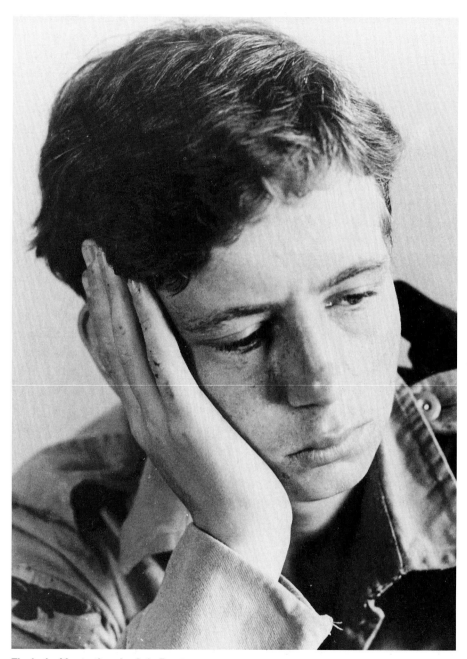

The look of frustration: Jamie in Egypt

nature of his style, and his capacity for melding his particular experience with social history and the narrative parameters of the cinema, put him strangely out of step with prevailing intellectual modes and practices in his native country.

Scotland's film academics, theorists and producers, unwittingly I suppose, found themselves keen bedfellows of the nationalist cultural landlords when it came to Bill Douglas. Like the New Town planners, they aimed to faze out anything which smacked of 'humanity' or social responsibility, acting like they were Modernism's inventors, smothering all with concrete definitions of their own. While writers from abroad, like the film critic of the *Statesman* of New Delhi, could see that the *Trilogy* 'ought to be of interest to the experimental film directors of India, and all those interested in the liberation of the human spirit', Scots critics discounted the films as negligible social realism. John Gibson wrote: 'It is ironic that the BFI Production Board, ostensibly dedicated to finance films that break new ground, should have invested so much money in Douglas's work. Not only is it not progressive, it crystallises the worst elements of a bankrupt tradition.' Such criticism was typical. The professional critics, for all their intellectual concerns, had come to the same conclusion as many of the Newcraighall locals: they didn't like the films because they were not 'progressive', they showed the community in a bad light. Douglas said:

> Ever since the first screening in 1972 I have made quite a few enemies. The films have been seen in Italy, Canada, Russia, Iran, China, America ... but curiously enough all the attacks have come from Scotland. I wanted to make a musical out of my childhood but somehow it didn't sound very tuneful. So I couldn't satisfy the Scot who asked me why I hadn't made a glamorous film, or the other who suggested I was drunk when I made them. ... My advice to future film-makers is not to embark on anything autobiographical unless they have a Hollywood-type background.

Agencies set up over the years to promote Scottish film, such as Films of Scotland, the Scottish Film Council and the Scottish Federation of Film Societies, have colluded with a governing enterprise ethos whose remit has been primarily to sell Scotland. By presenting an untroubling, sanitised picture of contemporary Scottish life, free of dissent and loaded with 'progressive' imagery (itself a thrusting technical bowdlerisation of the Grierson documentary tradition), these producers effectively continued with the romantic *pas de deux* of kilt and kail – all done under the superficial guise of a combative modernism. Some contributors to the 1982 collection *Scotch Reels*, a lame but influential book written by seven Marxists in search of a generic post-modern tribe, noticed the ways in which various styles and traditions had been brought together to promote the in-joke that was 'Scotland on the move'. Though all these critics were 'happy to polemicise on behalf of modernism', and to deconstruct some tartan myths, they failed to engage with film-makers who, under their noses, were trying to fuse naturalism with a critical modernism. To them, such as Douglas was just 'humanist realism' – the harbinger of a clapped-out style.

Ten years after *Scotch Reels*, certain Scots critics spoke of the guilt they felt in having failed to recognise Douglas's gift. This admission shows rare intellectual honesty; and, of course, the blame for cultural failure cannot be laid at the feet of individual critics. Yet the climate created by critical ignorance, on the one hand, and the British cinema's domination by consumerist zealots on the other, effectively killed the possibility of films being made which strayed from the twin ideological agendas of critical fashion and the film industry. When he died in 1991, Bill Douglas, despite international acclaim, had spent years trying to find backers for two remarkable scripts: an adaptation of Hogg's *Confessions of a Justified Sinner*, and *Flying Horse*, a film on the life and work of pioneer film-maker Eadweard Muybridge. Douglas said: 'If you've ever sent your script to STV and after a year didn't even get an acknowledgment or waited five years for money to make the film, you'll know why your obsession is the most precious thing you have.' It is possibly the one Scottish tradition most Scots artists can relate to: the one that, from Burns to the present day, has seen the best of Scotland's talent lie poor, ignored and humiliated, after five minutes of lionisation.

By 1927 there were 634 cinemas in Scotland, but there has never been an effective film production infrastructure. Scotland's daft and bonny cinematic grimace had been constructed, on the whole, by producers outside Scotland. A treasure trove of sickly melancholia and swashbuckling romance, ready-made for slick 'B' movie presentation, was culled from the seedier end of the national literature and plastered on to screens around the globe. Silents like *Rob Roy* (1911) and *The Call of the Pipes* (1917) made way for the later grandiloquent brain-damage that was *Brigadoon* (1954) and *Highlander* (1986). The debacle of the Scottish National Film Studios idea, put into action in 1946, demonstrates once more the spurious attempts of cultural nationalists to equate creativity with propaganda. They too were concerned with 'playing a not unimportant part in the coming revival of Scottish prosperity', aiming to educate young people into being 'creative artists and good Scots'. The studios closed in 1954, having succeeded in producing nothing but a short film on road safety. The Scottish Film

Production Fund, which has an annual production budget of just £150,000, has been very slow to initiate any diversity of film projects. They are hamstrung by a clear commitment to mainstream projects and 'professional work capable of appealing to substantial audiences'. *Living Apart Together*, *Venus Peter* and *Silent Scream*, all of which obtained some money from the fund, are fairly strong contemporary films, dealing with Scottish subjects in Scottish places. But these films are very much the exception. The Fund has signally failed to nourish talent and invention and has shown a penchant for slack teledrama. Ten years in operation, the Fund has not shown itself to be capable of laying the foundations of a small film community in Scotland, or even of promoting interest in Scottish cinema. One result of this has been the flood of film talent into television production.

The small-business and enterprise ethos of the Thatcher years tapped into a latent desire in many would-be independents to give it a go. Channel Four, the paradoxical child of this ethos, gave encouragement to Scottish independent television companies like Big Star in a Wee Picture and Gallus Besom to thrive in the private sector when all thoughts of a public sector film industry in Scotland are dead. The small companies were guaranteed an outlet for their work on the fourth channel and, since 1987, other channels have been committed to commissioning 25 per cent of output from independents. If the market likes them, they have a future. If, as in Bill Douglas's case, viewers and advertisers oust them from this highly competitive market, these artists will simply not be able to make pictures or programmes. Like the future of national health, the well-being of the national film culture has been increasingly exposed to the rat-race of the internal market, and priority will increasingly go to producers and directors who can produce the top dollar and the right viewing figures. Douglas's last film *Comrades* was closed in London after six weeks. The film was never given full distribution despite being the Critics' Choice of 1987. Commercial interests, of course, in the mid-80s often found themselves at one with the ideological temper of a philistine government.

John Berger has written that 'the powerful fear art, whatever its form, and among the people such art sometimes runs like a rumour and a legend because it makes sense of what life's brutalities cannot, a sense that unites us, for it is inseparable from a justice at last. Art, when it functions like this, becomes a meeting-place of the invincible, the irreducible, the enduring.' Such meeting-places are hard to come by, especially in a country which prefers the diversionary trapdoors and narcissistic one-way mirrors of cultural nationalism and cynical art theory to the small miracles of art. We may all be strangers and, if Coleridge can be believed, 'the largest part of mankind are nowhere greater strangers than at home.' Yet the cinema, this century's great invention, had often seemed like a medium which might offer a home to us all – a global homeland of the imagination.

The Young Film Maker of the Year Award at the 1991 Edinburgh Film Festival bore the name of Bill Douglas. It can only be hoped that the young directors who clutch it over the years find encouragement, and funding, to make the films they want to make. It is to be hoped, moreover, that they will suffer none of the neglect that followed Bill Douglas from his home in a small mining village near Edinburgh to the waiting rooms of the world's premier film financiers. And back.

When Bill Douglas's completed *Trilogy* opened in London at the end of the 1970s, the *Observer*'s film critic Philip French wrote that he believed it would come to be regarded 'not just as a milestone, but as one of the heroic achievements of the British cinema'. Whether it was a milestone remains to be seen; perhaps it is too individual, too painfully unique in its vision, to have that kind of relationship with the work around it. But of its heroism there can be no doubt; it is simply impossible to write about it without constant reference to the iron nerve, the determination, the stubborn faithfulness to a private vision, written into every image. Douglas's courage as a film-maker expresses itself powerfully in the films' style, particularly in the two earlier pieces *My Childhood* and *My Ain Folk*. The unrelieved austerity of the grainy monochrome images, the sparsity of the dialogue, the insistence on conveying the story through brief, allusive visual images rather than upfront verbal exposition, the deliberate use of unexpected camera angles and movements to carry meaning, the essential flatness of delivery in the dialogue, the refusal to make the actors act 'naturally' despite the apparent harsh realism of the background – are all bold stylistic decisions, perfectly attuned to the experience of childhood isolation and deprivation that Douglas wants to convey. There's something dry, powerful, almost Brechtian in the way the adult actors seem to 'indicate' their role in the child's story, rather than losing themselves in the subjective experience of their own characters.

> Some men have an image of what womanhood ought to be, and react violently against those who are vicious and cruel; they don't always want to know about the causes, some bleak and lamentable background.
>
> SHEILA HANCOCK
> ACTOR & DIRECTOR, JUNE 1992

But the *Trilogy*'s courageous style is fully matched, indeed shaped, by the boldness of its underlying theme. For it seems to me that Douglas's films confront one of the deepest taboos of this or any other culture, namely its capacity for neglecting and abusing its own children, its occasional complete failures of nurturing. There is probably not a culture on earth which does not have the capacity for some form of child abuse, whether it takes the form of neglect, emotional bullying, imposition of rigid social norms, sexual or economic exploitation, or plain physical brutality against those who are small and weak. But you have only to measure the self-righteous, explosive outrage of media and politicians every time such abuses are exposed in our own society, the furious, defensive self-distancing from failure or cruelty, to know how difficult we find it to face up to such failures, or to our own part in them.

And working-class communities in places like Scotland and the industrial north of England perhaps traditionally found this possibility of failure even harder to confront than most, if only because poverty and high mortality rates made family breakdowns an ever-present threat. We have, in Britain, a significant literature of cruelty to children, from Dickens onwards. But such writing often deteriorates into easy, sentimental dichotomies, between the 'poor little rich boy' sent off to boarding school on the one hand, and the warm-hearted poor on the other. The standard iconography of working-class community life, in Scotland as elsewhere in the industrialised world, is all to do with compensatory virtues of warmth and solidarity, with the innate decency and the family values that, in legend, kept the home fires burning and the doorsteps gleaming white even in the toughest times; with the sense that 'we', the workers, were more caring people, for all our poverty. It takes a brave man to drive a coach and horses of bitter memory through all that. Of course, says Douglas, some working-class families and communities may have functioned in that way; indeed we catch a faint echo of that world in the play of the other village children from which Douglas's little hero, Jamie, is always excluded. For example, we have the early scene where he watches the children running to meet their fathers coming up from the mine, and being cuddled and carried home. But Douglas focuses, relentlessly, on the grim underbelly of working-class life that those of us who can just recall that post-war, pre-affluence period are bound to recognise, like some long forgotten stench; on the ragged, smelly five-year-olds from the wrong side of the tracks who used to pee themselves in the classroom from sheer fright and immaturity; on the savage, visceral enmities that would blow up in closely packed working-class communities where emotions were never discussed, only occasionally allowed to explode; on people brutalised by brutal conditions, living lives without beauty in rootless communities that were little more than long-term labour camps, characterised as much by clannishness and competition as by sharing and solidarity, and ruthless in their exclusion of those at the margins.

And at the centre of this counterblast to the image of the unfailing warmth of working-class mythology is the sainted mother. We all know this figure, of course, the self-immolating tree-grows-in-Brooklyn matriarch who holds the family together by the strings of her frayed but spotless apron, the Mam, or Maw, or Momma, or Mamma, who feeds the whole family on broth or chicken soup for a shilling a week, keeps her kids decent with salvaged scraps of soap and the house gleaming with elbow grease, weakens her eyes darning shabby clothes far into the night, takes in washing, goes out cleaning, disciplines the kids, teaches them right from wrong, and brings them up respectable with precious little help from 'him', always unemployed or unhelpful, unfaithful, importunate or down at the boozer. This miracle-working mother, creating oases of warmth and order amid poverty and squalor, makes too many appearances in the literature of the industrial revolution and its aftermath to be dismissed as a pure figment of the imagination. There must, indeed, have been millions of women who worked, worried and starved themselves into an early grave trying to protect their children from the consequences of poverty, and the canonisation of such dead parents is almost inevitable.

But the idea that women can somehow be depended upon to produce this miracle of nurturing – that they possess some natural magic that enables them to make homes and care for children adequately regardless of physical or psycho-logical circumstances – is as improbable as it is sentimental, sexist and reaction-ary. And Bill Douglas's willingness to challenge it, particularly in his portrayal of Jamie's two grandmothers, is one of the most interesting and decisive aspects of his radicalism, as we can see if we consider the narrative of the early sections of the *Trilogy*.

At the point where the story begins, both Jamie and his older 'brother', Tommy, are already effectively parentless, and living with their old, worn-out grandmother, who is enmeshed in permanent mourning for her two lost daughters. Tommy's mother has just died, and his father is a ne'er-do-well from a neighbouring village who puts in rare appearances. Jamie's mother is in a mental asylum in Edinburgh; his father, a miner who lives across the street under the influence of his passionately possessive mother, does not acknowledge him. The old grandmother appears to love the boys, and to be loved in return. But she is more of a walking coffin than a human being, a long pillar of black clothing who spends most of her time immobile in her rocking chair, and is occasionally seized by a passion of demented grief which drives her away into the fields, where the boys find her cradling dead birds and keening. She has neither the resources to feed and clothe the boys properly, nor the emotional energy to talk to them; they are permanently starved, cold, ragged and filthy, stealing food where they can, burning sticks of furniture for warmth. After grandmother's death, things get even worse. Tommy is dragged fighting and screaming into a van and taken to a welfare home; Jamie, who has by this time formed an idea of his parentage, flees to his other grandmother's house, where he is avoided by his father, brutalised by his uncle, and – most terrifyingly – subjected to the meanness and violent mood swings of a passionate, driven old woman who alternately starves, bullies and (occasionally) pets him.

In other words, in developing his scenario Douglas flatly refuses to portray these two grandmothers either as superhuman figures, rising above the physical squalor and emotional bleakness of their surroundings to offer a loving home; or, for that matter, as 'wicked stepmothers' without redeeming features. Instead, he shows us two real women, old and sour, at the ends of their tethers, both in their different ways incapable of offering the child the attention and affection he needs. What the films do in a social context where such a recognition is quite unusual is to demonstrate that the grandmothers are not benign, passive, self-abnegating figures, but human beings, women with passions, needs and desires; and that where these are repressed and thwarted, violence and cruelty will result, as surely as in men. The suppression of emotional and sexual truth is, I think, a central theme of *My Childhood* and *My Ain Folk*, reflected in the loud texture of silence which Douglas creates around Jamie. His life is lived out in a miasma of unspoken knowledge, unmentionable facts, unacknowledged passions, feelings for which no one has a name; and even where adults do speak of these things, they always do so out of Jamie's earshot, or just on the edge of it. In this deep silence of emotional inarticulacy and repression, the child becomes tremendously observant, searching diligently for clues about the emotional subtext of his life and relationships, finding them often particularly in the movement of people's hands, the tense clasp of his maternal grandmother's cold hands as she rocks and grieves, the ferocious fist his paternal grandmother makes on the arm of her chair when she talks about Jamie's mother 'destroying' her precious son's life, the menacing twirl of her thumbs before she rises up and lunges towards her son's mistress with the bread knife, or the imperious hand she stretches backwards for Jamie in the moments when she wants company and support.

But it has to be recognised that the profound silence and lack of verbal articulation is not just a conspiracy against the child. It is written into the culture Douglas is describing, where language is used sparingly and tentatively, feelings – particularly tender or sexual feelings – are rarely brought into the open and named, and unexpressed tensions tend to erupt into sudden, implacable hatreds; and it is clear that the women, as much as the men, are the carriers and victims of this repressive culture. Hence, I think, the tremendous pent-up violence that seems to lurk in the personalities of both Jamie's grandmothers. His maternal grandmother is the less extreme case. Her central passion is love for her daughters

The 'good' granny: Jean Taylor Smith

and grief at their loss; and although her old woman's lack of self-control in failing to protect her grandsons from her despair deviates from the norm of 'motherly' reassurance (there is something terrible and memorable about the early scene where she lies in bed beside Jamie weeping openly for her 'girls'), the feelings themselves are unexceptionable. Even here, though, there is a terrible latent fury, directed against the men who have used and abused her daughters. When Tommy's father appears on the boy's birthday, bearing a canary in a cage as a present, the grandmother's face – in Jean Taylor Smith's magnificent performance – briefly takes on a wild flash of superstitious fear, followed by a closed, mulish hatred. She throws the man out of the house in a selfish passion of hatred, quite indifferent to the pain she is causing the distraught Tommy, who has never had a chance to meet his father; and later, in a despairing, vengeful rage, she pulls the canary cage down from its hook and begins to savage it, wildly, with a broom-handle, as if it were the man himself. Later, on her way to visit Jamie's mother in the asylum, she stops and spits, vehemently, at the door of his paternal grand-mother who dismissed Jamie's mother as a whore.

But the maternal grandmother's trembling desire to hurt where she has been hurt is as nothing to the perpetual repressed rage of Jamie's relatively well-to-do other grandmother, who sits by a small fire barking out instructions, forbidding Jamie to sully the indoor toilet by using it, drawing lines on milk bottles so the boy shall not dare to drink, and giving short measure, both sexual and nu-tritional, to everyone except her adored elder son. In Helena Gloag's performance – tiny earrings, tense body, face by turns hard-bitten and strangely girlish – this is a formidable portrait of a passionate woman helplessly frustrated, her energy perverted into a sour, life-denying negativity. The camera lingers on her yearning body language as she caresses and worships her elder son ('she was a whore, son, you're a king' is her refrain, as she dismisses yet another girlfriend); it stares in fascination at her tense, menacing hand movements as she suddenly vents her fury at the latest 'whore', or holds a trembling Jamie in a vice-like grip to pour out her bile at her husband's relationship with a village woman, declaring with bitter, destroyed pride that she 'never let him touch me, not once'. And even more alarming than her violence is the terrible clutching tenderness she sometimes lavishes on the child, once when she is drunk, and then again after she has sat, cold-faced, watching her younger son beat the boy to a whimpering pulp. 'Yer grannie loves you,' she intones exaltedly, a dozen times; but the boy senses that this greedy, self-serving possessiveness, alternating with spasms of cruelty and rejection, is only a crippled parody of love.

Now it seems to me, as a woman, a feminist, and a Scot, that these portrayals of Jamie's grandmothers, ugly though they often are, are truthful and necessary and immensely powerful. Douglas's meticulous truthfulness, as an artist, enables him to cut through the idealisation/demonisation of women that is the failure to perceive them as rounded human beings, with their own complex needs – which too often dogs the work of male artists; he is not interested in the madonna–whore dichotomy, and his women cannot be placed within it. Instead, he utterly fulfils the demand implicit in the quotation from Sheila Hancock with which I began this essay: that men face up to the fact that women are not made of sweetness and light, and that they do so not by recoiling from the uglier faces of womanhood, but by looking at 'the causes' from which such ugliness emerges. In his detailed characterisation of Jamie's grandmothers, Douglas draws the most powerful and persuasive connections between the physical and emotional poverty of these women's lives and their failure to nurture the child physically and emotionally; between the sexual and emotional repressiveness of the culture which surrounds them and the viciousness of the pent-up emotions which they vent on the child. And in drawing out these patterns, he not only looks into the heart of a sour truth about Scotland's dour and emotionally grudging culture, but also illuminates, in a much wider sense, the way in which emotional violence and deprivation perpetuate themselves from generation to generation, often – and this is what both male sentimentalists and romantic feminists must face – through the female line.

There does, however, remain one legitimate question mark to Douglas's handling of women in the *Trilogy*, and that concerns the overall balance of the films as an account of a failure in nurturing. That Jamie's two grannies fail him, in their different ways, is clear; but the films have less to say about the initial trauma of fatherlessness, of illegitimacy and total paternal deprivation, which has formed the basic pattern of Jamie's character and sexuality before the story begins. It is a common observation that all the characters in the *Trilogy* with whom Jamie forms positive relationships are male: the German prisoner-of-war Helmut, the paternal grandfather, the boys' home superintendent, and finally the army friend Robert; and in psychological and artistic terms this is easy enough to understand. Jamie has suffered the pain of fatherlessness since infancy, and his real father, when his identity finally becomes clear, is self-indulgent, evasive, a dead loss. Small wonder that the impulsion of the narrative comes from the boy's search for a replacement; small wonder that his erotic drive focuses upon it. In this basic psychodrama, the women are part of the background, not central players.

But perhaps because Douglas is not able to handle this theme of homoeroticism and its roots explicitly enough, the result is a slight skewing of his vision.

Apart from the haunting glimpses of thwarted beauty and possibility in the portrayals of the two grandmothers, the women in the *Trilogy* partake totally of Douglas's bleakness. The minor characterisations of Jamie's father's blowsy mistress, of the stepmother he later marries, of the grandfather's mistress, of the shut-faced schoolteachers, of the hospital nurse who viciously pockets Jamie's apple on his single visit to his mother, are all touched by a harsh and almost gratuitous ugliness or absurdity; whereas at least some of the men Jamie meets are gilded by this softer light of yearning, this sense of redeeming possibilities for loveliness and fulfilment behind the bleakness of everyday things.

In other words, the camera in Bill Douglas's hands does not yearn for women as it yearns for men, or perceive their potential in the same way. Having stripped them of the false, sanitised magic of the 'sainted mother', it can barely sense the real, erotic magic that makes them lovely again, although sometimes it sees the outer shapes and patterns of it; and the *Trilogy* might have been more perfect, more wholly satisfying, if Douglas had been able to confront that fact, implicitly recognising the possibility of other erotic sensibilities in confidently acknowledging his own. But that slight twist, that exclusion of women from the resolution of the *Trilogy* and the upward movement that leads to it, is a small price to pay for the profound understanding Douglas brings to the two principal female characters, and the extent to which he acknowledges their driven, complex, suffering humanity. In Sheila Hancock's words, he is not afraid to contemplate the 'bleak and lamentable background' that shapes their paths, or to recognise how it twists and stunts female lives as deeply and destructively as male ones. And for that, all of us who are tired of being virgins or whores, perfect mothers or wicked stepmothers, good wives or bad girls, anything at all but real women with inner lives as complex and ambiguous as any man's, have reason to be grateful.

Peter Jewell, Bill Douglas's friend and companion, relates that Bill's interest during his last days centred on gardening. It seems that he had turned away from film. He had at last freed himself from the grip of those images which beckoned, tantalised and tormented him.

In the sense that Zanuck said of Renoir that he was 'not one of us', Bill Douglas was never a *professional* film-maker. Which is why the industry, whatever that was or is, never backed him. How can you deal with a man who will not compromise, who doesn't understand what the word 'career' means or care what the future brings so long as he gets the next shot right? How can you trust a man whom you cannot bribe with 'You'll cry all the way to the bank', or threaten with 'You'll never work again'?

In his last years he tried to understand what investors, commissioning editors and the like wanted. He began to sound like everybody else: yes, he wanted to make an entertaining film; no, it would not be inaccessible; yes, he would make changes; no, it would not be expensive; yes, he would stay within budget. Somehow none of it sounded convincing. Not because it wasn't true, but because it wasn't relevant. Turning himself into a plausible producer was not going to be the answer. The fact was that his film mattered to him more than life itself. Negotiation was possible – just – but not guaranteed. The only real dialogue that Bill seriously entertained was about the audience. I know this will surprise people who find aspects of his films obscure or distant, but he saw his job as keeping the audience held and stretched. He was determined not to insult or bore – which is perhaps the same thing. Questions about audience perception of a scene or structure would draw him out. I cannot recall him, when challenged, not having a view of where the audience would find itself in a shot or cut. He did not hide behind 'it just feels right'. He would explain. So much for the myth of Bill Douglas the primitive and intuitive artist.

Bill gave me the impression that he did not create the images which he put on paper. They came to him. Sometimes after a struggle but more often freely and inexorably. That is why he resisted interfering with a scene out of context. He saw it as forcing rather than receiving. If he was persuaded to change something on page forty he would start revision with that change in mind on page one. Often the process led to changes en route. This way of working explains why his scripts are *organic*. I have often wondered whether that was the reason he found the editing process so difficult: that he needed to go from the beginning to sense whether a new cut or order was right. Bill's style of shooting and construction was particularly dependent on cutting and rhythm and yet, strangely, he was unsure in the cutting room and needed help.

Experience was not of much use when tackling Bill's films. The material was so volatile that a few frames either way changed not only the rhythm but the meaning. The most difficult to judge were the reaction shots. Even to call them that is misleading. In a world of silences they signified action as much as reaction. Behind the impassive faces there was rage, contemplation, fascination, confusion and more. Sometimes the meaning changed and evolved during the life of a shot of an apparently unchanging expression. If it was timed short for narrative then the scene was diminished, if longer then tension was lost. As I said, the difference sometimes amounted to frames. In *My Childhood*, the scene of the German POWs waiting in the lorry while the guard was pissing was originally cut long and emphasised his control; Kevin Brownlow cut it slightly faster, which had the effect of making the scene feel more habitual and routine and threw emphasis on Jamie and Helmut later in the sequence. Sometimes Bill could articulate the problem without knowing the solution. In *My Ain Folk* he was unhappy with the sync sound recorded in the exterior shot of a van driving away from camera with Tommy inside looking out of the back window. Although the shot was an objective one, Bill wanted the audience to get inside Tommy's head. Mike Ellis, now one of Britain's best editors, was the sound editor and he came up with the idea of turning the magnetic film upside down so as to read the sound through the cel side. We ended with an exterior picture and a muffled interior sound suggesting Tommy's state of mind.

When I established the Directing Department at the National Film and Television School in 1977, I invited Bill to teach there. As a member of the BFI's Production Board, Colin Young, the School's principal, had supported Bill strongly and was keen to have him there. (But he had his reservations about the *Trilogy*: he asked Bill, 'Why doesn't Jamie go to the fitba? After all, admissions are free for the last twenty minutes of a game!') I had doubts about Bill's temperament for the job. He could be uncommunicative and, as he was self-educated, I wondered whether he had the patience. Still, I felt I should give him a try because he was despondent that not a single offer had come his way after the *Trilogy* and he was flat broke.

Bill was a success. Teaching revealed his sunny side. He was as open as a teacher as he was secretive as a film-maker. During the making of *My Ain Folk*, for example, they were shooting outside Jamie's 'old' home. His father's brother was smashing the furniture looking for Jamie's mother's pearls and throwing the pitiful fragments on to a bonfire outside. I overheard this conversation between Gale Tattersall, the cameraman, and Bill.

'Bill, does this scene cut with the one we did the other day?'

'Why do you ask?'

'If it does, you've broken the eye-line.'

'What's it got to do with you? You're not the editor.'

'I was only trying to be helpful ...'

'Stick to being the cameraman.'

He may sound like a tyrant but he believed that every person – actor or crew – should be responsible for their part and nothing more. That there should be one director and not many directors pulling this way and that. In fact, he valued Gale as cameraman and asked him to shoot *Comrades*, which he did brilliantly.

When Bill was at the NFTS he wrote a script for a students' exercise. His brief was to write a story with five scenes to be shot in as many days, in which the students alternated roles as director/editor, cameraman, sound recordist, production manager and designer. Dialogue was to be kept to a minimum. The result was 'Frank and Millie', which described the break-up of a relationship. The five lines of dialogue were: 'Frank,' 'Frank', 'Millie', 'Millie' and 'Millie'. It is a piece that many experienced directors would have relished. Bill gave the students the freedom and space that he himself wished as a film-maker. He did not instruct or dictate, instead he waited for the students to come up with the ideas. He gave them the confidence to trust their instincts. His approach was direct: be true to what you see inside your head; reject what is not essential – what you leave out is as important as what you put in; don't show the audience something it can imagine better than you can show it. His teaching was about the constant interplay between seeing and being seen, between the subjective and the objective. With most film-makers there is hardly any relationship between what they do, which is often haphazard, and what they say, which is invariably well-formed. Bill the film-maker and Bill the teacher were all of a piece. One illuminated the other.

When Bill suggested bringing actors to the School for acting workshops, I was surprised. Although he had trained as an actor, I thought he was, professionally speaking, against actors. I had seen him on the set of *My Childhood* and *My Ain Folk* giving the most simple directions, blocking in the action and very little else. It was difficult to reconcile his method with his training under Joan Littlewood, that arch neo-Stanislavskian. Not only did he not encourage discussion, he deepened the mystery by not giving the scripts to the actors. Even the leads got their own pages and nothing more, and sometimes only on the day. So how did he get those wonderful performances? One tends to look for explanation by examining technique and method. In Bill's case that would be to avoid looking at something more ineffable: his character and psychological make-up. To be on a

Bill Douglas scene – 'set' is too artificial – was to be in a place where people worked in a focused and determined way. Individuals were free to give of their best, and the results cohered. They added up, more or less, to Bill's view. I do not know how. I speak here with certainty only of the two shoots that I witnessed, on *My Childhood* and *My Ain Folk*.

More conversationally, actors and crew members will talk about trust. They trusted him to make the best use of their talents. They trusted him to join what they had all given him into a significant film. Few have been disappointed, although one or two may have struggled more. Trust, after all, cuts both ways. Jo Blatchley, who played Robert (Peter Jewell in real life) in *My Way Home*, wanted Bill to trust him. In the sequence where Robert is sitting on the sand and Jamie comes up to him, Bill wanted Jo to draw an X with his finger in the sand, draw another X and point at Jamie and draw a line between the two Xs. Bill gave very precise directions for when Jo should look up, draw and so on. Jo asked for a rehearsal to get the action right. Bill raged against that, saying he didn't want a performance; he wanted it real. Every rehearsal and every take pushed the actor away from reality. Jo suggested that Bill should trust the actor to find his way towards the truth. Anyway, Jo didn't get the sequence of actions right in the first take. So he got his rehearsal after all.

On the one occasion I saw Bill handling a crowd, I realised how much he worked from how things *looked*. He was setting up the shot in *My Ain Folk* of the miners entering the pit cage. He told the group nearest the cage to start to move slowly forward after counting five from 'Action'; the group behind was to move after eight, the one behind that after ten and the last group after eleven. What we see in the film is an uncoordinated body of miners, lumbering and stupefied by exhaustion. Bill had achieved this effect without once referring to motivation or meaning.

For the workshops at the NFTS, Bill adopted a more Stanislavskian approach. There was an agreement with the actors that he would not spring things on them but might create surprising situations. The difference is subtle and again has to do with trust. Three particular actors, I recall, generously gave themselves to these experiments: Bill Russell, Kate Scofield and Rob Pember. They had fun and games. Kate Scofield was told that she was going to a tryst with her lover and arrived to find Bill Russell eating a meal with his 'son' – of whose existence she was not aware – and not taking any notice of her. Bill was given lines of dialogue with a child and found, to his recorded horror, that the boy took out a bag of sweets and concentrated on that. But the actors also learnt a few things. They all say they became better *screen* actors. The students, including Ian

Knox, Carlo Gebler and Oliver Stapleton, speak of Bill with affection and respect. Away from the demands of film-making, Bill, who was essentially a very shy person, allowed his warmth to emerge. His time at the NFTS, in the midst of his frustrated attempts to make films and earn a living, was one of the periods which he enjoyed.

Recently I sat on a selection panel for directors at the NFTS. Ian Sellar, who trained on Bill's films and at the NFTS, was another panel member. We were both surprised and impressed by the number of applicants who named Bill as an inspiration and an influence. It could be that they had done their research, but I doubted they'd known of my connection as I do not have a credit on any of Bill's films (that's another story). In any case, I challenged them to be specific about what they admired. One of them, Ashleigh Irving, singled out a scene from *My Childhood*. She described it in this way: 'There was this shot of some flowers in a mug. Although they were droopy, they were the only thing of beauty in the whole place. Shockingly, Jamie comes in and throws away the flowers and pours boiling water into the mug until the water overflows on to the table. He then empties the mug and puts it between the cupped hands of his grandmother. He holds her hands and pats them. And then I realised that there was something much more beautiful than the flowers.' Ian Sellar leant forward transfixed. His eyes were wide open and moist. Twenty years earlier he had found these very poppies. Bill had looked at them and, without a word, had taken out his cigarette lighter and played a flame under the flowers until they had wilted and dropped. Then he arranged them in the mug.

Bill Douglas's last resting place, Bishops Tawton Churchyard, Devon, 1992

PHOTOGRAPH: REBECCA RUSSELL

CHARLIE CHAPLIN'S LONDON
London Film School, 1969, 16mm (lost)

STRIPTEASE
London Film School, 1969

Credits: Bill Douglas, Steven R. Edwards,
Bill Hodgson, George Thomas,
Mike Tinter.

Cast
Verity Bargate.

Running time: 5 mins. 35mm.

GLOBE
London Film School (undated)

Running time: 1 min. 16mm.

COME DANCING
London Film School, 1970

Direction/Script: Bill Douglas.
Production: Temmi Lopez.
Editing: Hasnath Majumdar.
Asst. Editor: Bill Hodgson.
Sound: Jack Gardner.
Camera: Hassan Sharock.
Lighting: Mel Puig.

Cast
Clive Merrison, Michael Elwick,
Nicole Anderson, Verity Bargate.

Running time: 15 mins. 16mm.

MY CHILDHOOD (1972)

Director/Writer: Bill Douglas. Producer: Geoffrey Evans. Cameraman: Mick Campbell. Editor: Brand Thumin. Sound Recordist: Bob Withey. Sound Editor: Tony Lewis. Additional Photography: Gale Tattersall, Bahram Manocheri. Sound Mixer: Mike Billings. Asst. Cameraman: Roger Pratt. Continuity: Ian Sellar. Asst. Director: Nick Moes. Production Company: British Film Institute.

Cast

Stephen Archibald (*Jamie*), Hughie Restorick (*Tommy*), Jean Taylor Smith (*Grandmother*), Karl Fieseler (*Helmut*), Bernard McKenna (*Tommy's father, Mr Brown*), Paul Kermack (*Jamie's father, Mr Knox*), Helena Gloag (*Father's mother, Mrs Knox*), Ann Smith (*Jamie's mother*), Eileen McCallum (*Nurse*), Helen Crummy (*Teacher*), Helen Rae (*Bus Conductress*), James Eccles (*Man singing*).

Running time: 48 mins. 16mm.

Prizes won

1972 Chicago: Silver Hugo for Best Student Film.
1972 Mannheim: Der Preis der Katholischen Filmarbeit.
1972 Nyon: Sesterce d'Argent.
1972 Venice: Silver Lion, Premio di Selezione Venezia Critici.
1972 Writers Guild of Great Britain: Best British Original Screenplay.
1973 Montreal: Diplome d'Excellence.
1973 Tehran: Special Prize, Film Critics of Tehran Publications, Best Short Film, Extra Gold Plaque of the Jury.

MY AIN FOLK (1973)

Director/Writer: Bill Douglas. Producer: Nick Nascht. Asst. Producers: Charles Rees, Tony Bicat. Cameraman: Gale Tattersall. Editor: Peter West. Assembly Editor: Brand Thumin. Sound Recordist: Peter Harvey. Sound Editors: Peter West, Michael Ellis. Dubbing Mixer: Doug Turner. Property: Elsie Restorick. Asst. Cameraman: Bob Taylor. Asst. Director: Ian Sellar. Personal Assistant: Gordon Craig. Production Assistant: Roderick Farquharson. Production Company: British Film Institute.

Cast

Stephen Archibald (*Jamie*), Hughie Restorick (*Tommy*), Jean Taylor Smith (*Grandmother*), Bernard McKenna (*Tommy's father, Mr Brown*), Mr Munro (*Jamie's grandfather, Old Mr Knox*), Paul Kermack (*Jamie's father, Mr Knox*), Helena Gloag (*Father's mother, Mrs Knox*), Jessie Combe (*Father's wife, Agnes*), William Carroll (*Father's son, Archie*), Anne McLeod (*Father's girlfriend, Helen*), Robert Hendry (*Soldier, John*), Miss Cameron (*Schoolteacher*), John Downie (*Undertaker*).

Running time: 55 mins. 35mm.

Prizes won

1974 Cork: Silver Medal Craft Award for best cinematography.
1974 Edinburgh: Interfilm Jury Recommendation.
1974 Nyon: Prix spécial du Jury des Jeunes.
1975 Prix Sadoul (ex aequo).

MY WAY HOME (1978)

Director/Writer: Bill Douglas. Production Supervision: Richard Craven, Judy Cottam. Cameraman: Ray Orton. Sound Recording: Digby Rumsey. Editor: Mick Audsley. Dubbing Editor: Peter Harvey. Dubbing Mixer: Doug Turner. Camera Assistants: Bob Taylor, Jeff Strasburg, Steve Shaw, Abdul and Ali. Asst. Director: Martin Turner. Production Assistants: Bob Settle, Celia Southerst, Fatima Rateb, Mr Safwat. Production Help: Hag Shaffrey. Continuity: Keith Silva. Art Direction: Oliver Bouchier, Elsie Restorick. Production Company: British Film Institute.

Cast

Stephen Archibald (*Jamie*), Paul Kermack (*Jamie's father, Mr Knox*), Jessie Combe (*Father's wife, Agnes*), William Carroll (*Their son, Archie*), Morag McNee (*Father's girlfriend, Helen*), Lennox Milne (*Grandmother*), Gerald James (*Mr Bridge*), Andrew (*Boy in Home*), John Young (*Shop assistant*), Ian Spowart (*Schoolboy*), Sheila Scott (*Foster mother*), Rebecca Haddick (*Salvation Army woman*), Archie (*Down and out*), Joseph Blatchley (*Robert*), Radir (*Egyptian boy*), Lita Roza (*Singer*), William Russell (*Voice of Sergeant*).

Running time: 72 mins. 35mm.

Prizes won

1978 Chicago: Bronze Hugo.
1979 Berlin: Fipresci Prize.

THE BILL DOUGLAS TRILOGY (My Childhood, My Ain Folk, My Way Home)

Prizes won

1979 Antwerp: Critics Prize.
1979 Berlin: Interfilm Jury Special Prize.

COMRADES (1987)

Director/Writer: Bill Douglas. Producer: Simon Relph. Associate Producers: David Hannay, Redmond Morris. Production Managers: Donna Grey, Charles Hannah. Production Co-ordinator: Deborah Carter. Lighting Camera: Gale Tattersall. Stills Producer: David Appleby. Editor: Mick Audsley. Production Designer: Michael Pickwoad. Costume Designers: Doreen Watkinson, Bruce Finlayson. Make-up Artist: Elaine Carew. Composers: Hans Werner Henze, David Graham. Script Editor: Peter Jewell. Production Company: Skreba, in association with the National Film Finance Corporation, Film Four International and Curzon Film Distributors.

Cast

Alex Norton (*Lanternist, Sgt. Bell, Diorama Showman, Usher, Wollaston, Ranger, Tramp, Captain, McCallum, Silhouettist, Mad Photographer, Witch*), Robin Soans (*George Loveless*), Imelda Staunton (*Betsy Loveless*), Amber Wilkinson (*Hetty Loveless*), William Gaminara (*James Loveless*), Katy Behean (*Sarah Loveless*), Stephen Bateman (*Old Tom Stanfield*), Sandra Voe (*Diana Stanfield*), Philip Davis (*Young Stanfield*), Valerie Whittington (*Elvi Stanfield*), Harriet Doyle (*Charity Stanfield*), Patrick Field (*John Hammett*), Heather Page (*Bridget Hammett*), Keith Allen (*James Hammett*), Patricia Healy (*Mrs Brine*), Jeremy Flynn (*Brine*), Shane Down (*Joseph Brine*), Robert Stephens (*Frampton*), Joanna David (*Mrs Frampton*), Michael Hordern (*Pitt*), Freddie Jones (*Vicar*), Barbara Windsor (*Mrs Wetham*), Murray Melvin (*Clerk*), Dave Atkins (*Foreman*), Collette Barker (*Servant girl*), Michael Clark (*Sailor*), Alex McCrindle (*Gaoler*), Jack Chissick (*Constable*), Sarah Reed (*Blonde girl*), Nicola Hayward (*Dark girl*), Mark Brown (*Legg*), Vanessa Redgrave (*Mrs Carlyle*), James Fox (*Norfolk*), Arthur Dignam (*The Fop*), John Hargreaves (*The Convict*), Symon Parsonage (*Charlie*), Charles Yunipingu (*Lone Aborigine*), Simone Landis (*Flower*), Anna Volska (*Woman in white*), Brian McDermott (*Auctioneer*), Shane Briant (*Official at burial*), Tim Eliot (*Registrar*), David Netheim (*Police officer*), Ralph Cotterill (*Bertie the guard*), David McWilliams (*Digger*), Lynette Curran (*Whore*).

Running time: 183 mins. 35mm.

Prizes won

1986 London Film Festival: BFI Sutherland Trophy.

HOME AND AWAY (1974)
Director: Michael Alexander.
Writers: Bill Douglas, Michael Alexander.
Photography: Mark Littlewood.
Editor: Charles Rees.
Production Company: British Film
Institute.

Cast
Barry Malone, Malcolm Reading,
Margaret Alexander, Michael Malone.

Running time: 31 mins. 16mm.

THE TRILOGY - ON VIDEO

MY CHILDHOOD/MY AIN FOLK
CR 064   RRP £14.99

MY WAY HOME
CR 065   RRP £14.99

CONNOISSEUR VIDEO SPECIAL OFFER